# KIENHOLZ

# KIENHOLZ
## THE HOERENGRACHT

ED AND NANCY
REDDIN KIENHOLZ

JANUARY 15 – FEBRUARY 25, 2002

534 WEST 25TH STREET
NEW YORK, NY 10001

PaceWildenstein

Edward Kienholz had been making rough-and-ready, down-and-dirty assemblages, many of them sexually provocative reinventions of the human form, for seven years when he produced his first environment. That seminal piece, *Roxys* (1961-62), set the tone for the ambitious tableaux he continued to make until his death in 1994, both on his own, and from 1972 on, in collaboration with his wife, Nancy Reddin Kienholz. Although it takes its name from a notorious brothel in Las Vegas, *Roxys* was actually based on his recollection of a visit to a whorehouse in Kellogg, Idaho, as an adolescent, which he recalled in 1977 as an appalling experience: "a bunch of old women with sagging breasts that were supposed to turn you on."[1] Kienholz's honesty in speaking about such usually unmentionable matters was of course embedded in the art he made. Even when the social criticism is at its most pointed, he resisted the temptation to point the finger at others, choosing instead to admit to his own failings and vulnerability.

This recourse to the subjectivity of his own temperament, even at the risk of presenting himself in an unflattering light, contributed to the immense authority of the work Kienholz made throughout his life, first independently and then with Nancy Reddin Kienholz. Fearless about the possibility of exposing their own weaknesses, unwilling to censor even their darkest thoughts, and comfortable about addressing themselves to delicate issues that many couples would leave unspoken even in private, they created for themselves an enviable freedom to make art grounded in the most urgent issues that face us. Among their themes one can number loneliness, isolation, and social interaction; mental instability, old age, and mortality; racism and fear of otherness; pretense, piety, and religious fervor; mindless patriotism; copulation, procreation, and prostitution. Which other artists in our time have addressed themselves to such a wide range of difficult and profound subjects? Perhaps only among literary figures could one find an equivalent. And it is not just in terms of subject matter that the Kienholzes distinguished themselves. Add to this the visual and practical inventiveness with which they reshaped their vision of the world, using fragments of real things as basic working materials, and one can begin to understand why their place in postwar art history is such a special one.

The moral dimension of the Kienholzes' art always carries with it an understanding of the need to accept one's own foibles and to take responsibility for one's own actions. *All Have Sinned in Rm. 323* (1992) addresses the theme of dirty thoughts behind closed doors. It represents a woman slumped back in licentious abandon, naked below the waist, her legs spread wide open in front of a television set. Above the TV is an ostentatious display of pious Christian paintings and sculptures. The tableau constitutes a savage and undisguised attack on the hypocrisy of the religious right and particularly of those televangelists who preach chastity while secretly paying for the services of prostitutes. But there is a note, too, of sympathy even in the title itself, which recognizes that these sinful thoughts might be the artists' own—and ours as well. The title and idea for the work came from a "misreading" of a road sign with the biblical passage "All have sinned. Romans 3:23." In this context the more sympathetic reading of the work calls to mind another biblical dictum: Jesus saying, to those jeering at the woman taken in adultery, "Let he who is without sin cast the first stone."

Like the individual figure sculptures that had preceded it, *Roxys* is life-size. Even though it takes huge liberties in the representation of the figure, this human scale encourages an immediate visceral identification from the spectator that gives the scene a strong sense of realism. In this case the viewer is kept on the outside looking in, but the conception of the piece as a complete room, a world coherent in itself, establishes an essential operating principle of Kienholz's art, one which implicates the viewer as a participant, with all the psychic disturbances that this involvement entails. The artist's eye for telling detail is everywhere apparent, the potent evidence accumulating like the vivid flashbacks of a shocking experience haunting his "remembrance of things past." After inhabiting a Kienholz space, viewers add their own impressions to their personal memory bank. The effect can vary wildly, depending on individual sensibilities: it can be oddly comforting, like a return to the womb, or deeply disturbing, even traumatic, like an event buried deep in the mind that suddenly surfaces as a perhaps unwelcome visitor to consciousness.

The entire room presented in *Roxys*, from the patterned wallpaper down to the well-worn carpet, acquires the exaggerated immediacy of the scene of a crime assessed by a sharp-eyed detective with a lifetime's knowledge of human behavior. Every object seems to tell its own part of the story. The choice of furniture and other found objects is deliberate, designed to recreate a highly particular sense of time and place and establish a strong atmosphere that animates every object, turning each chair or sofa into the site of some lustful assignation. Half a century earlier, Marcel Duchamp had devised the first ready-mades as an escape from the artist's role as creator; he had insisted on his neutrality as a way of avoiding the stranglehold of aesthetic judgments and welcoming the arbitrariness of an object plucked almost at random from the world. While making use of the language of objects added to the vocabulary of sculpture by Duchamp, Kienholz reversed the procedure by scavenging with great care and undisguised subjectivity in order to select only those objects that could engage in some kind of conversation with one another. The overt theatricality of Kienholz's installations, together with the sense of narrative this engendered, could not have been more at odds with the art of its time. When first exhibited, the installations must have seemed as alien to the transcendental ideals of the Abstract Expressionists of the older generation as they did to the cool tenor and studied indifference of the emerging Pop artists.

In *Roxys*, the outmoded seats and cushions, the overstocked dressing table, the ugly table lamps and their cream-colored lampshades might strike one at first as theatrical props that convey the kind of existence lived out in a squalid environment, a place where frustrated men satisfy their lusts through women who make their bodies available in exchange for money. Prolonged exposure to this arena of fantasy tinged with nightmare, however, charges the inanimate objects with the same sense of life as the grotesque figures that inhabit the space, especially given the way the women are themselves constructed largely from things. Take "Five Dollar Billy," for example, lying passively and vulnerably naked, flat on her back, on top of an old wrought-iron sewing-machine table, like a mannequin waiting to be stitched up. She is more like a corpse, or like a woman undergoing an abortion, than someone anticipating the pleasure of sex. The Surrealists' fondness for a phrase in the Comte de Lautréamont's *Chants de Maldoror*—which described something being as "beautiful as the chance meeting of a sewing machine and an umbrella on a dissecting table"—seems here transmuted into a more terrifying, but equally potent, conjunction of disparate elements. Kienholz certainly can be seen as an heir to Surrealism, in relation particularly to the search for a "convulsive" beauty arising from unexpected associations deeply rooted in the psyche.

The violence of Kienholz's imagery, which extends also to the brutal way in which the paint is applied like blood to other figures, insists that we wake up to hard realities that we otherwise ignore. Controversial subject matter and shock tactics were not employed by the Kienholzes, as they were by some young artists in the 1990s, as a way of getting noticed or of offending middle-class sensibilities. It was more a howl of rage at the appalling things of which "civilized" human beings—and that means all of us—are capable. In this respect their work can be compared at least as usefully to that of Francis Bacon, with his powerful paintings of the human figure in rapture and torment, as to that of a much younger British artist, Sarah Lucas, whose funky, funny, highly sexual and ostentatiously vulgar sculptures can be understood partly as a legacy of the language pioneered by Kienholz before she was even born.

*The Hoerengracht* (1984-88), one of the last environmental pieces made by Kienholz and his wife prior to his death in 1994, harks back directly to *Roxys* in its subject matter. It is presented here for the first time in New York.[2] Also on view, within a normally hidden chamber intended for the storage of the packing crates, are eight of the fifteen *Drawings for The Hoerengracht*, created by the artists between 1984 and 1988 out of leftover elements they had collected for the main piece. Each of these reliefs, conceived in a similar spirit to the walk-in tableau as assemblages of found and constructed objects, exists as a highly condensed fragment of the same red-light district.[3]

Given the presence of "working girls" on the streets of Chelsea, the West Side district of Manhattan in which *The Hoerengracht* is now being presented, the ever-present dialogue between art and life in the work of the Kienholzes takes on a special urgency. Implicit to the piece, moreover, particularly because of its extremely ambitious scale, is a questioning of the artists' role in relation to the commodification of their work. In the need to make a living, to produce objects for the delectation of others, are their "pure" aesthetic motivations somehow sullied? Do artists in effect prostitute themselves by operating within the gallery system, or even—as in the case of this immense sculpture—when they make very large works that are difficult to accommodate except in museums? These may be tangential and unspoken questions, but they, too, beg to be heard as part of the context and meaning of the work. It would certainly not be the first time that Kienholz fed such issues into his art: in the 1960s he began two sets of watercolors, to each of which he added a large, rubber-stamped declaration of its value, either in terms of the consumer item for which it was traded (as in the case of *For a Monte Factor Suit*, 1969) or of the price that was set for otherwise identical works (ranging from *For $1.00* to *For $10,000.00*).

*The Hoerengracht* was constructed over a four-year period in Berlin, where the Kienholzes began living part-time in 1973, using large-scale photographs, fragments of real buildings, and elements hand-crafted by the artists. As with Ed's first environment, it was prompted by his experience of a particular place, in this case the official red-light district of Amsterdam, a favorite haunt of backpackers, tourists, and of course businessmen in search of sexual satisfaction. No one who has ever been there can fail to have been struck by the display of women of all ages, heavily made-up and sometimes dressed in little more than their underwear, standing in doorways or sitting at the windows of their small rooms under garishly colored lighting, flaunting their bodies and looking for business. The street as an arena of sexual fantasy and the satisfaction of physical desires proves a potent outlet for one of the abiding themes of the Kienholzes' work: the public expression of private thoughts.

For some men, this street theater offers a spectacle of pure tit-illation more arousing than anything they might find on stage in a strip-tease joint; for others, it acts as a sad and disturbing reminder of the exploitation of human beings and of the desperation that drives both the women who sell their bodies and the men who pay for them. Each of us, when wandering through such a place, may experience widely conflicting emotions—as we do when viewing this sculpture, which reflects with such honesty and accuracy both the look and the atmosphere of the open-air flesh market from which it derives. There is, moreover, no sense of escape. Once you enter into these five claustrophobic, narrow streets, cunningly worked into a floor plan measuring just over 43 x 23 feet, you descend into a vision of Hell or Purgatory (though to some, admittedly, it might seem like Heaven). There is a sense of being simultaneously indoors and out, of feeling protected while still being at the mercy of the elements and other people in the street. Walter Benjamin long ago described the relationship between street life, prostitution, and the narrow streets of Paris as a kind of open-air interior. As early as 1913, he had written about the feeling of being shielded by the city's boulevards, which he thought of as corridors because of the continuous walls formed by the uniform facades of houses that "do not seem made to be lived in, but are like stone sets for people to walk between."[4]

In view of the strong theatrical component of Kienholz environments since the early 1960s, the street theater of Amsterdam's brothel district, where each prostitute is displayed through the windows of her ground-floor room on a stage set of her own design, provided the artists with a compelling ready-made subject. Certainly this is one of the most visually alluring of their sculptures, with a strong formal structure subdivided into numerous sections, each complete in itself and each in turn opening up into a detailed private fantasy world. You apprehend its subject at first sight, but then are invited to experience it physically over time. As you walk through the space, you occasionally linger or find yourself distracted by something seen from the corner of your eye, as you would on the street itself. In a short text about this work published in 2001, Nancy Reddin Kienholz revealed that "Ed said he wanted to build this piece because the lights from the windows are so beautiful," but she added bluntly (and with caustic wit) as a parenthetical aside: "I never believed that."[5]

The mixed signals sent out by *The Hoerengracht*—the very title of which ("the whores' canal") puns on the actual name of one of the major Amsterdam canals, the Herengracht ("the gentlemen's canal")—shuttles us uncomfortably back and forth from pleasure and beauty to revulsion and squalor, from the freedom of unrestrained libido to feelings of guilt and disgust. As with *Woman Washing with Scrutator* (1985), a more compact environment made during the same period, the focus on a sexually available woman places the viewer explicitly in a voyeuristic role. There is no possibility of having a "correct" response, politically or otherwise, since one is confronted with one's own human complexities and contradictions. We enter the space at its widest point before being lured, out of curiosity, down the narrow alleyways. There we are made to run the gauntlet of whores' rooms, under the watchful stare of eleven women corresponding to different types and pieced together, like Brides of Frankenstein, from fragments of body casts and the heads of shop-window dummies.[6] At one point we meet a man in a raincoat who strides in our direction and whom, because he seems to the same size as us, we might mistake for a real person; the colored surface on which he materializes, which we momentarily take to be an immense mirror, is in fact a photograph. In our confusion, we expect to see our own reflection there, implicating us as participants or at least as peeping toms.

The women in *The Hoerengracht* exist in their separate spaces, silent, alone, as if in solitary confinement. Each figure takes the form of a sculptural object of reverence, mostly seated or otherwise raised on altar-like plinths in shrines decked out as temples of kitsch. Each woman's head is both shielded by and encased in a metal frame folded open, so that we approach it as a three-dimensional picture within a picture: a face to be gazed at with the intensity normally reserved for a beautifully designed object or work of art. Each of these faces in turn seems to scrutinize us, with an imperious expression that says, "Don't judge me."

The squalid, dirty, and used look of the buildings, and the tastelessness of the garish interiors, convey an atmosphere of sordid sexuality, of lust filled with shame and remorse. In a potent metaphor of psychological forces, uncontrolled animal desires are channeled into dark recesses at the margins of society. The tunnel-like spaces become the visual and physical equivalent of the secret corners of the mind itself, giving material form to the repressed desires that erupt suddenly when the opportunity presents itself. Taking shape as a labyrinth, the street promises both mystery and danger around every corner. In this sense, the street becomes the equivalent of the unconscious wandering into perilous areas that the conscious mind would rather keep at a safe distance. Even when we are supposedly focused on serious or everyday matters, it seems that the biological imperative keeps getting in the way. An oft-quoted statistic maintains that the interval between sexual thoughts in an average adult male is no more than a few seconds.

Few men, even in today's liberal climate, admit to using the services of prostitutes. A young man, in a burst of bravado, may brag about such exploits to his friends, but for older men to speak of paying for sex carries the stigma of inadequacy and sexual frustration, or an admission that the light of desire has been extinguished from a marriage. Street-level prostitution is of course viewed as the grubbiest and most wretched end of the market, especially now that even family newspapers carry ads for "escorts" and that call girls can be procured by telephone or over the Internet. In those areas of big cities where young girls in microskirts and older women in brassy "open-all-hours" attire stand, with legs suggestively spread, as they tout for customers, the business of sex-for-money may be out in the open, but an air of menace, risk, and suspicion still clings to every participant. The officially tolerated brothels of Amsterdam, with their frank display of sexual wares on offer, provide a more open and presumably more civilized model for the hiring of women's bodies by men. Even if one views all prostitution as a form of (mutual) exploitation, at least this open model understands the situation as a contract entered into willingly by both parties. It also has the virtue of accepting such behavior as a fact of life and the inevitable product of human nature. Simply by representing such an environment in their art, according it the dignity of their attention, the Kienholzes make a powerful political statement, unafraid of the controversy that might be provoked by their willingness to address truths that polite society would prefer remained unspoken.

Overt depictions of sexuality have become ever more prevalent in contemporary art since the 1980s. The graphic displays of copulation and extreme practices in Robert Mapplethorpe's photographs, the photo-screenprinted canvases on which a naked Jeff Koons displays himself penetrating his equally exposed wife, Tracey Emin's confessions of compulsive and anonymous sex in drawings evocative of public-toilet graffiti, and the fantasies of dirty sex enacted by Mike Kelley and Paul McCarthy are among many examples of this tendency to thrust into our faces sexual imagery that would once have been regarded as unacceptable or pornographic. For some artists, such motifs have served as a way of keeping their distance from a safe, stifling, middle-of-the-road audience. There is, of course, an honorable tradition at work here, rooted in the early days of modernism, for which we still use a French term: "épater les bourgeois." At the Paris Salon of 1865, Edouard Manet's presentation of his nude courtesan under the title of *Olympia* so enraged some visitors that it had to be hung high off the ground to prevent it from being attacked. (Today, of course, it hangs at the Musée d'Orsay in Paris, under the gaze of millions of visitors, who parade before it without complaint.) By the end of the nineteenth century, Edgar Degas and Henri de Toulouse-Lautrec were painting brothel scenes with a frankness that might once have shocked but which we can more easily accept today as a simple fact of life, particularly given the strong aura of high art that now envelops their work.

In time, *The Hoerengracht*—one of the great late environments by one of the pioneers of installation art—may come to seem just as matter-of-fact as these late nineteenth-century treatments of the subject of prostitution. Right now, thanks to its contemporary frame of reference, the realism of its setting, and the confrontational physical presence of the life-size three-dimensional figures, *The Hoerengracht* is very "in your face"—and deliberately so. But only the faint of heart are likely to find it offensive or deliberately provocative. Rather than setting out to shock, the artists who conceived and made this environment could be described as wishing—in the well-chosen words of another artistic partnership, the British artists Gilbert & George—to "de-shock," to normalize aspects of life and human nature previously ignored or regarded as taboo. As with all the art of Edward and Nancy Reddin Kienholz, the "whoroscope" of human behavior in *The Hoerengracht*—part analysis and part prediction, with a dose of horror and plenty of whores—is filled with love and compassion, pathos and humor: a piece of the world we have made for ourselves, reflected back at us in all its glorious imperfection.

NOTES

*With apologies to the late Samuel Beckett, whose first publication, *Whoroscope,* appeared in 1930, three years after the birth of Edward Kienholz.

1. Quoted in Robert L. Pincus, *On a Scale That Competes with the World: The Art of Edward and Nancy Reddin Kienholz* (Berkeley: University of California Press, 1990), p. 24.

2. There was insufficient space to include *The Hoerengracht* in the Whitney Museum's 1996 presentation of the touring Kienholz retrospective. It was, however, displayed in the Berlin showing at the Berlinische Galerie, Landesmuseum für Moderne Kunst, the following year, and reproduced in the American edition of the catalogue, *Kienholz: A Retrospective*, exh. cat. (New York: Whitney Museum of American Art, 1996), pp. 216-21, with a note by Rosetta Brooks.

3. For the most comprehensive account of the artists' "tableau drawings," see *Kienholz: Tableau Drawings Retrospective*, exh. cat. (Venice, California: L.A. Louver Gallery, 2001), and my essay on pp. 86-95. Specific reference to the *Drawings* for *The Hoerengracht* is made on pp. 93-94.

4. Quoted in Hannah Arendt's introduction to *Walter Benjamin: Illuminations* (London: Fontana/Collins, 1973), p. 20.

5. Quoted in *Kienholz: Tableau Drawings*, p. 62.

6. The women are named and described in detail by William Wilson in *Edward and Nancy Reddin Kienholz: The Hoerengracht*, exh. cat. (San Diego: Museum of Contemporary Art, 1993), pp. 17 and 21. As Wilson remarks, "Eleven figures that make up the cast dimly suggest the sexual archetypes of standard skinflicks from Nursey to Dominatrix. But the Kienholzes have so tenderly nuanced their characterization they cease to be merely living fetishes."

# THE HOERENGRACHT

**1984 – 1988**
**120" x 520" x 280"**

Tableau:
wood, plaster casts, clothing,
furniture, brick, concrete, steel,
lumber, sheetrock, wallpaper,
paint, curtains, plexiglass, leaves,
beer cans, bicycles, lights, radios,
stuffed dog, wigs, cardboard
boxes, sinks, carpeting, vinyl,
jewelry, magazines, telephones,
household furnishings, paint,
and polyester resin.

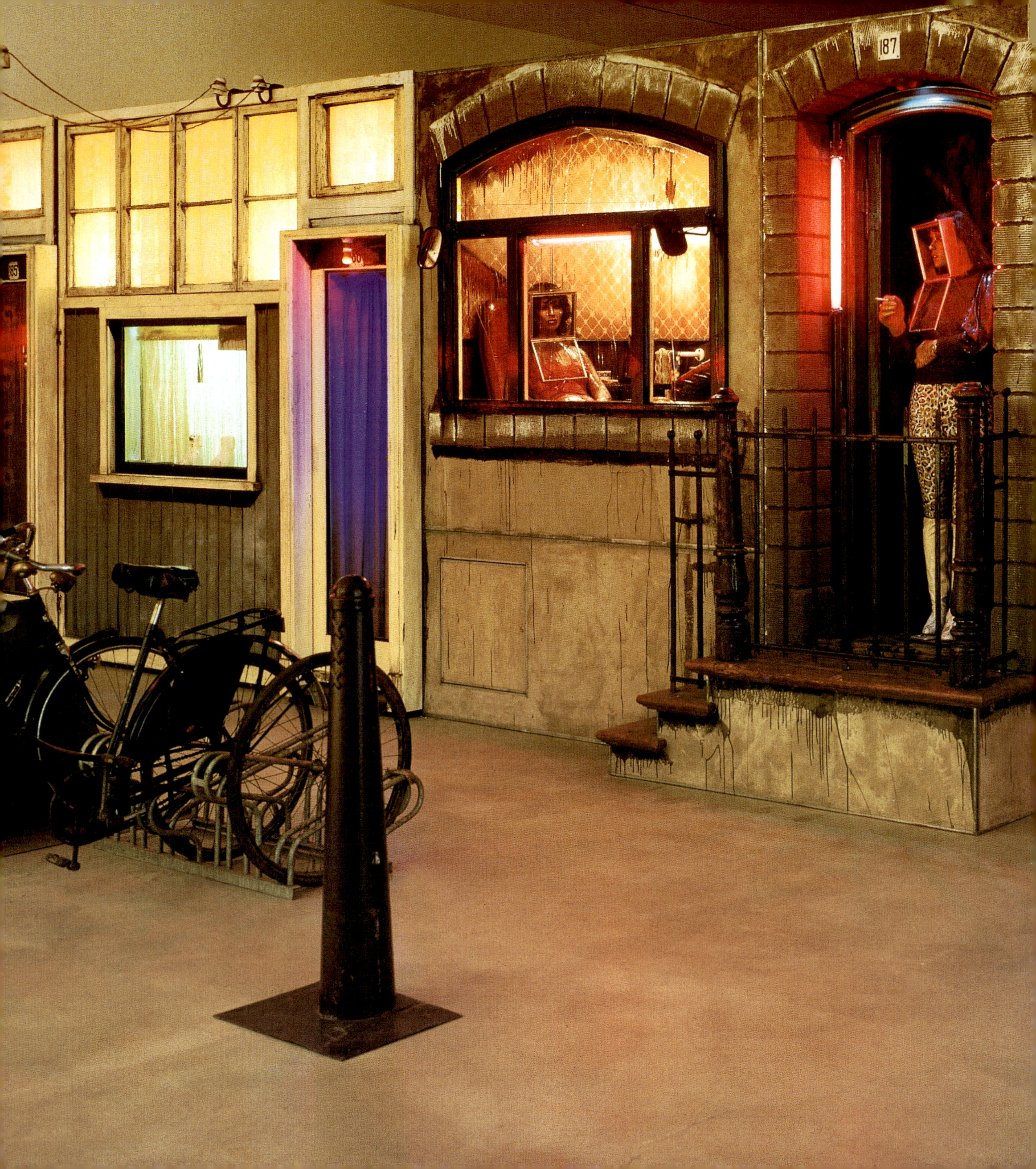

187

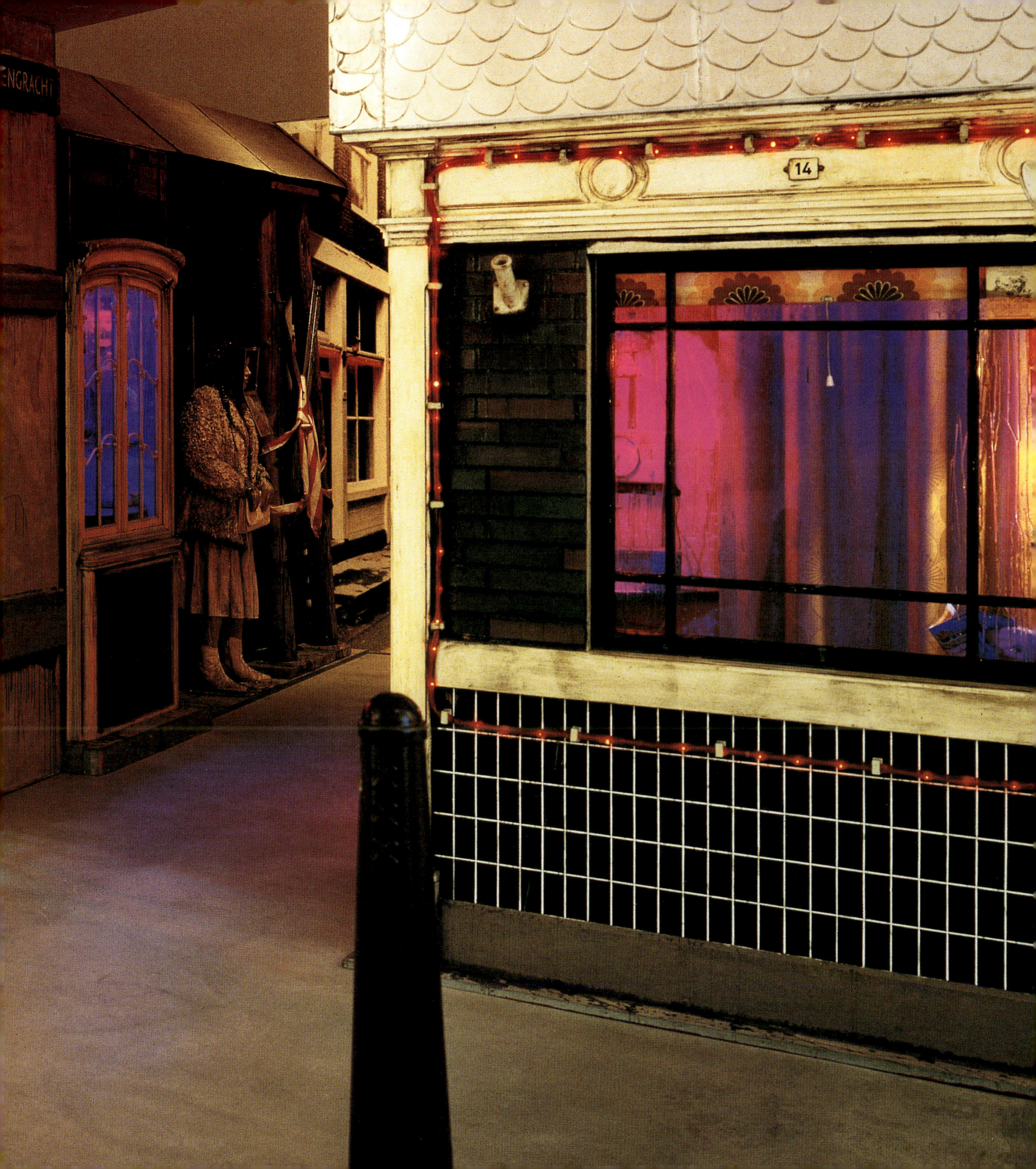
ENGRACHT
14

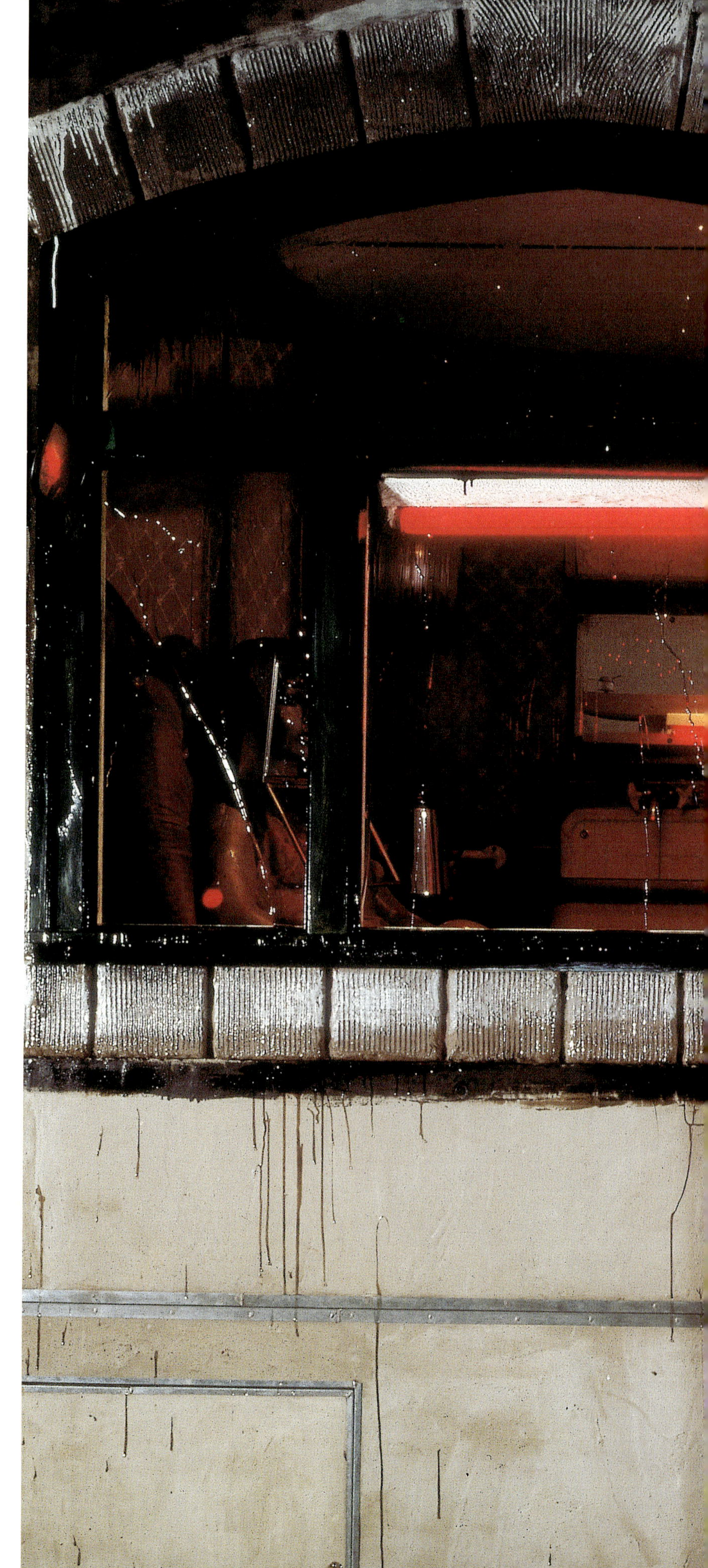

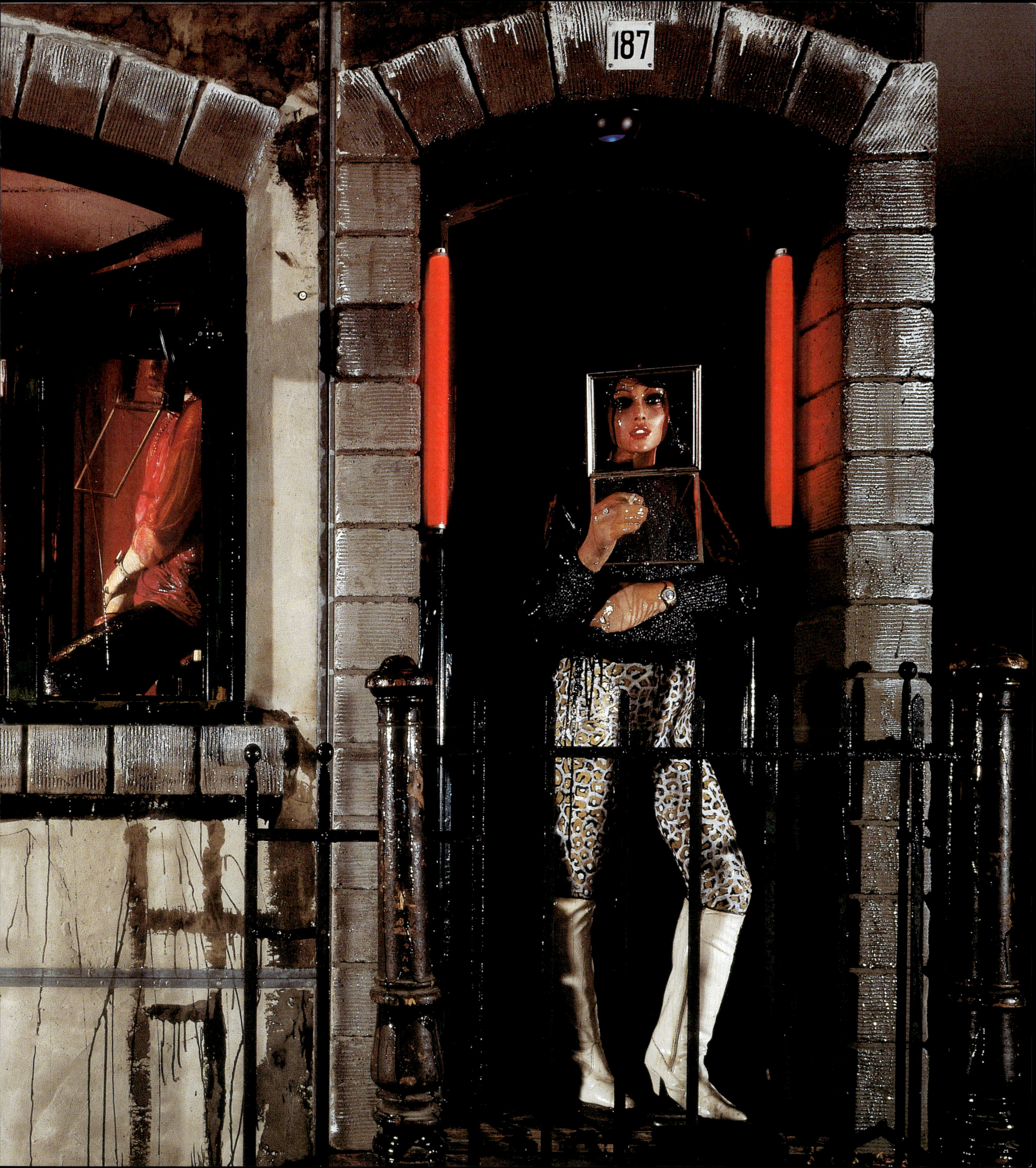
187

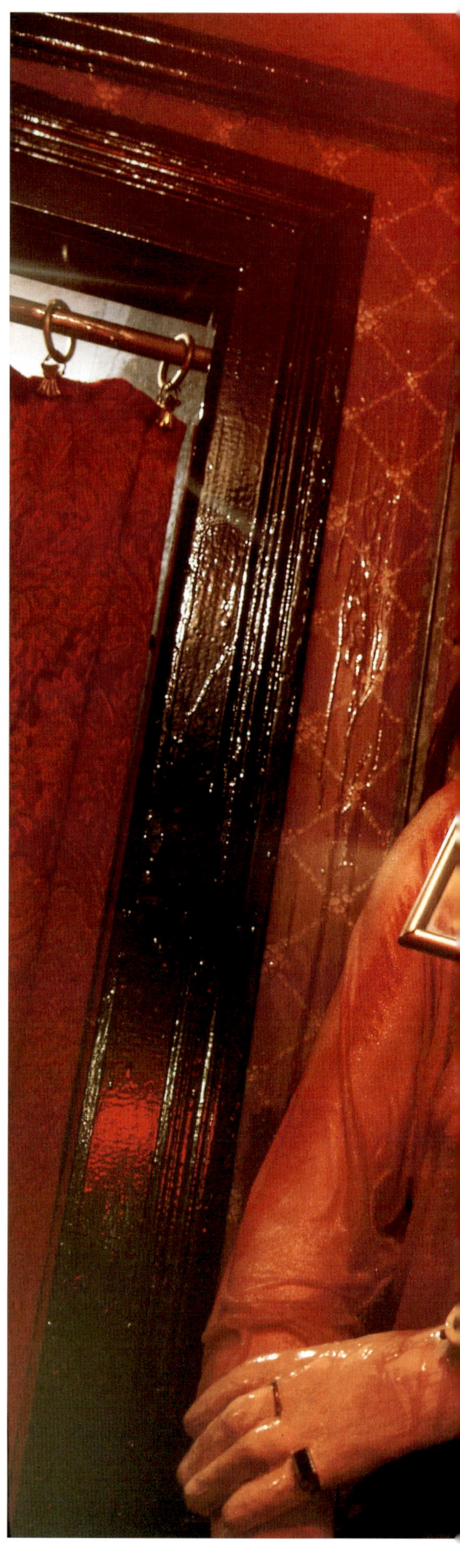

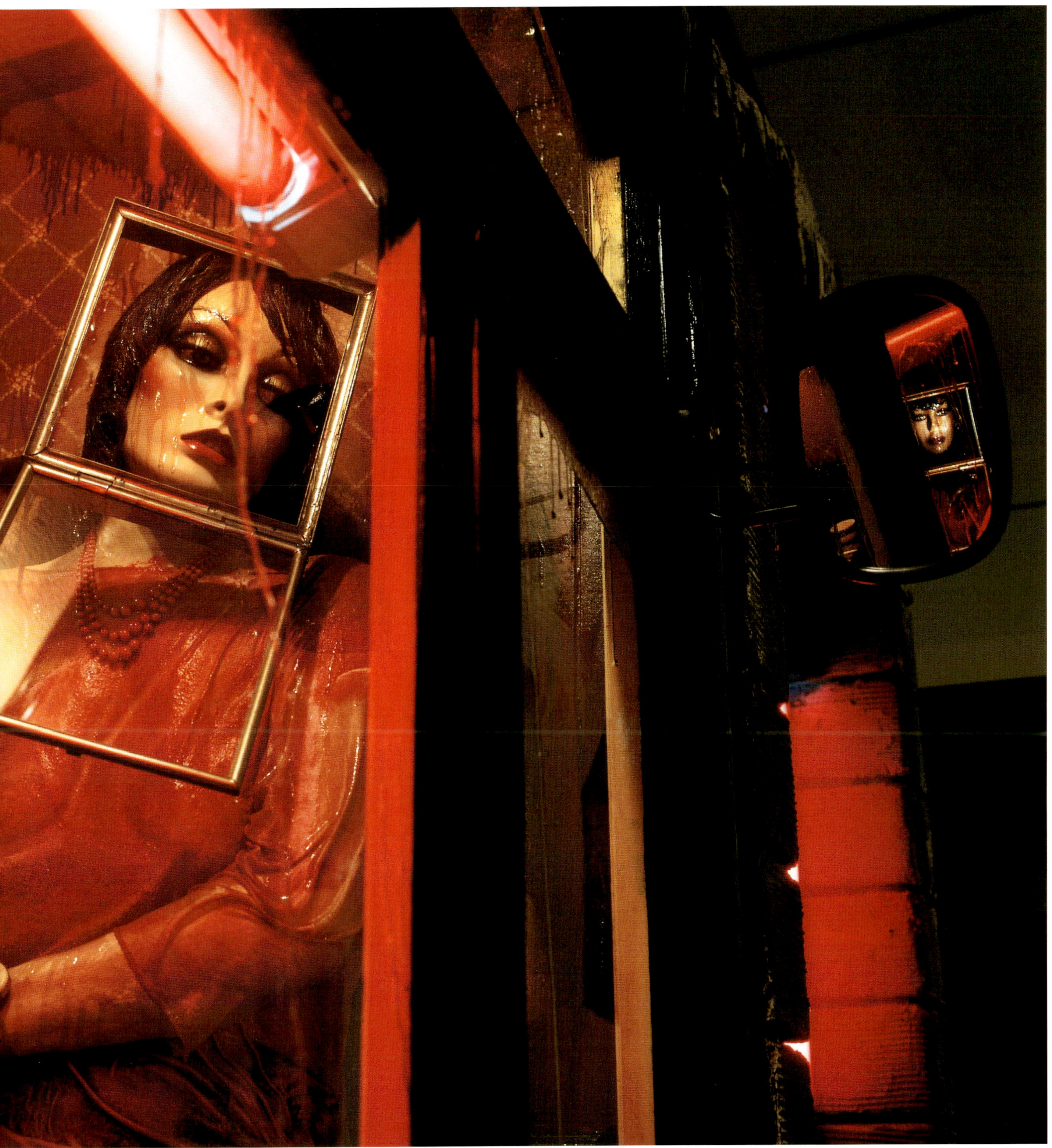

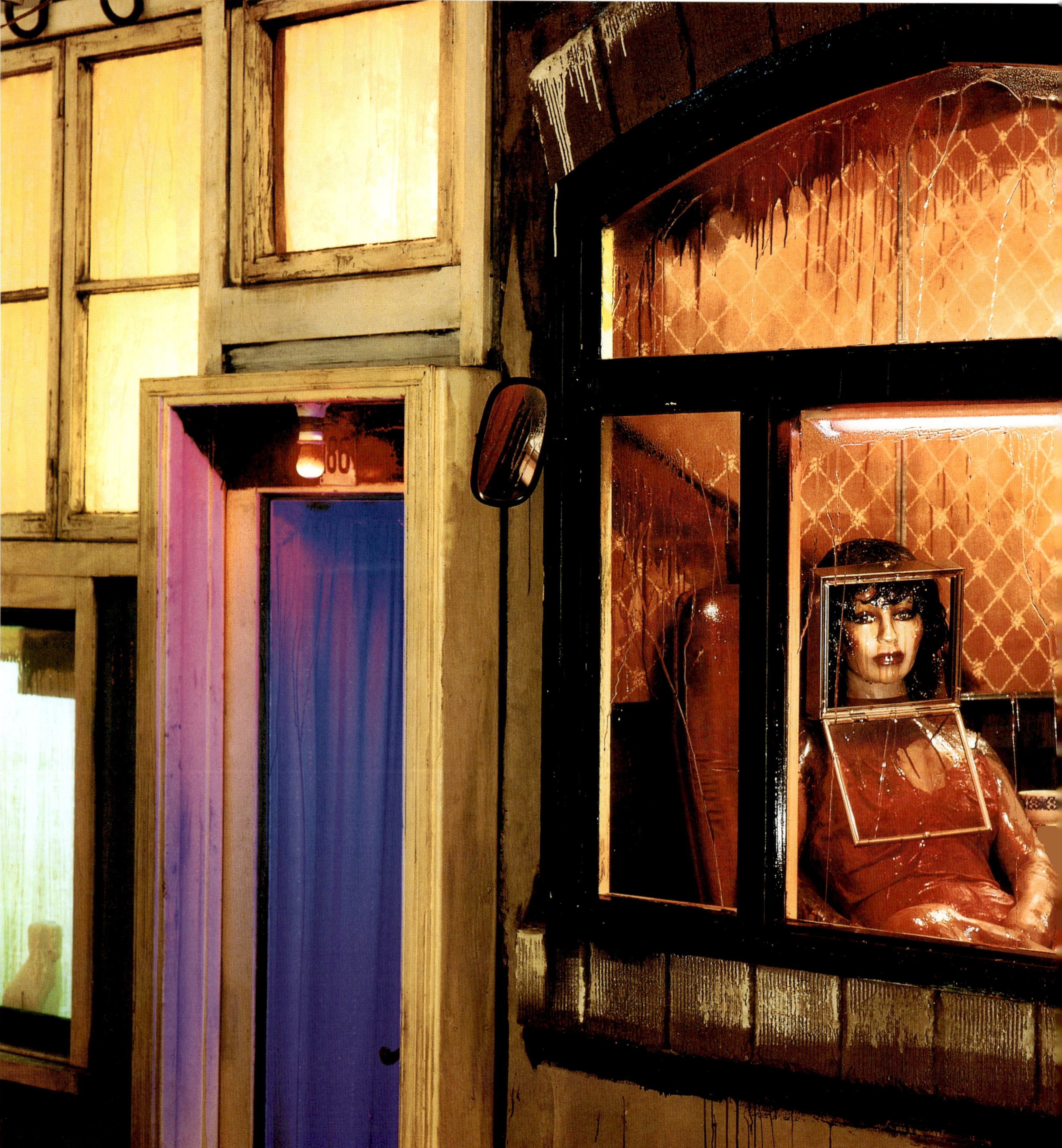

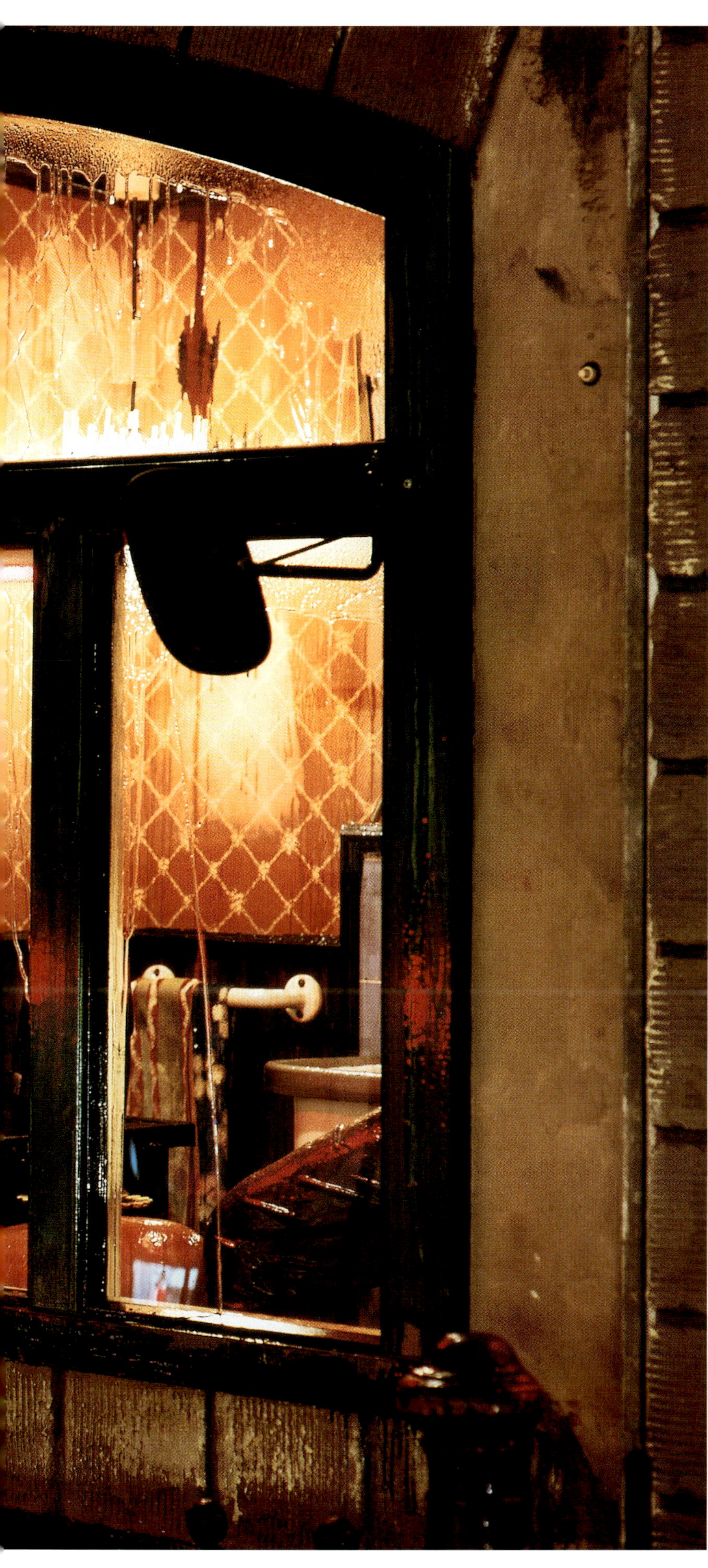

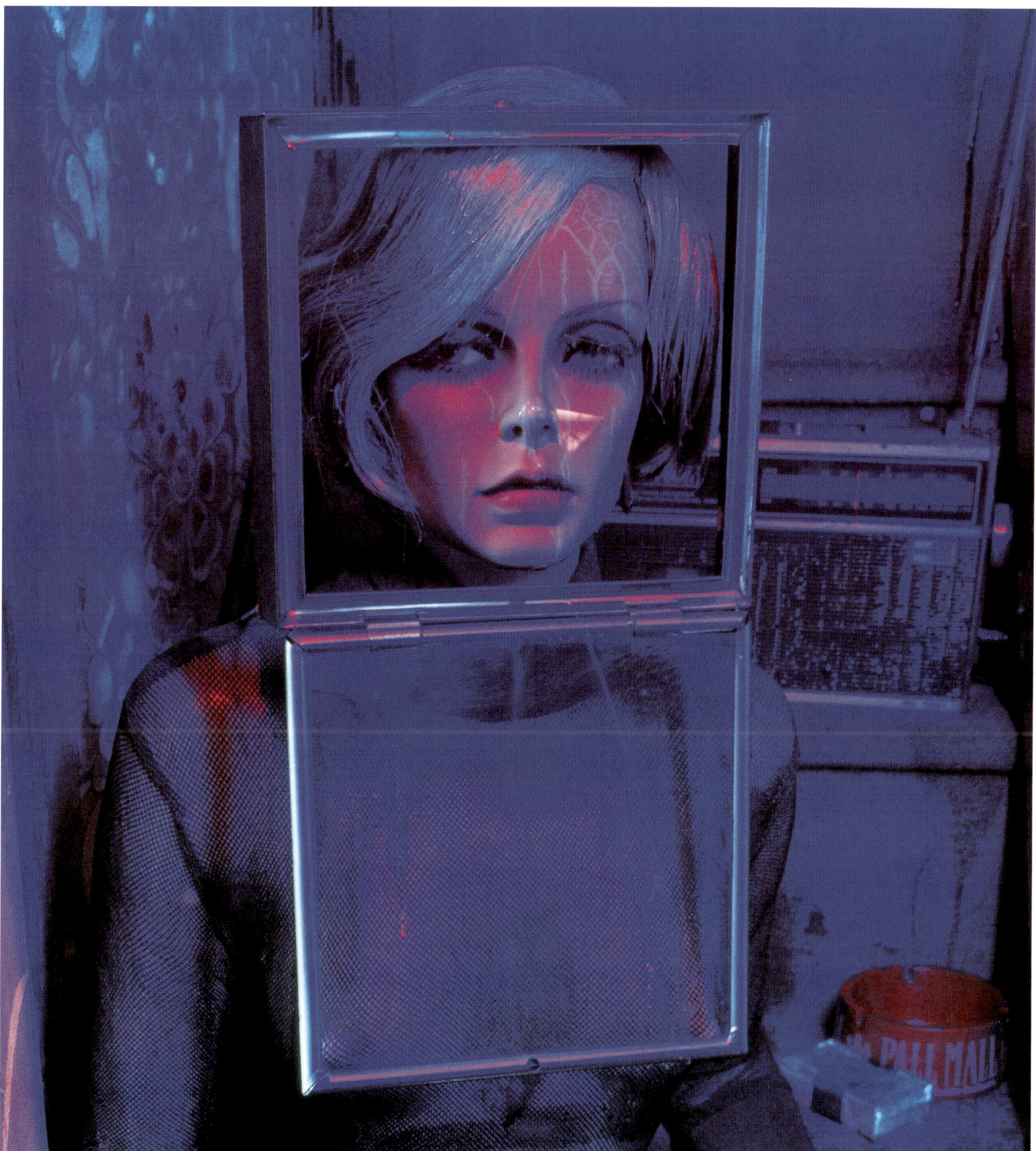

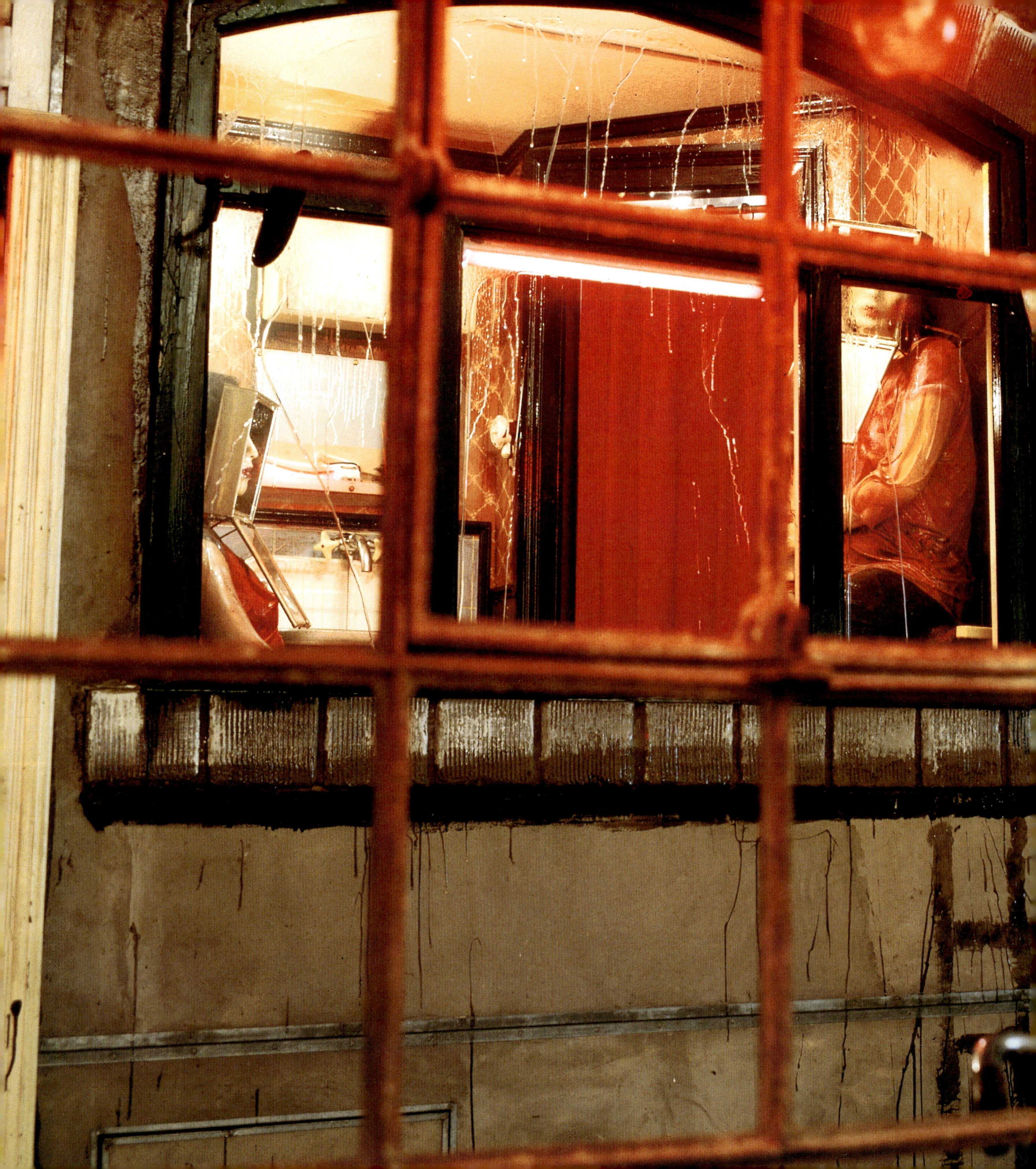

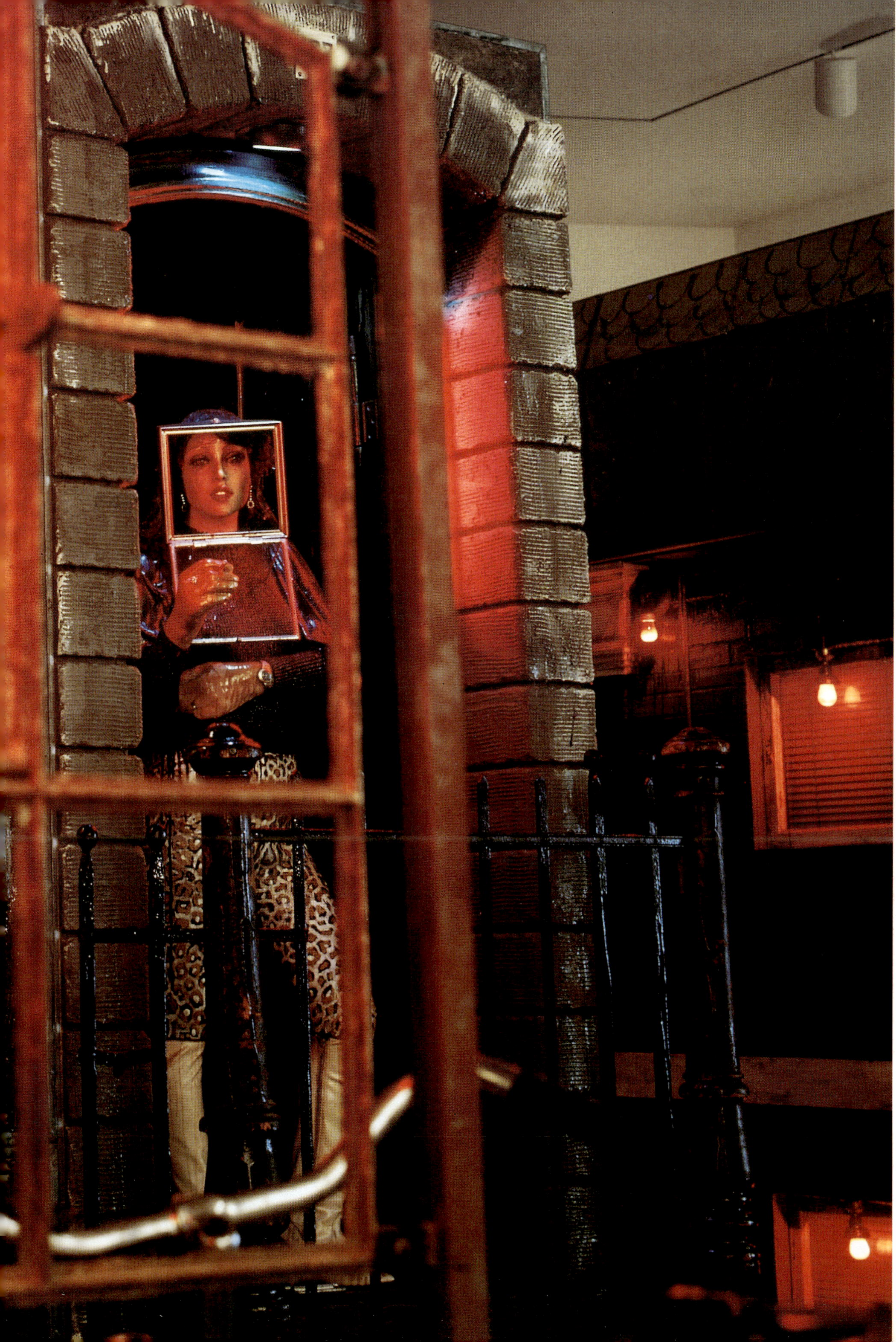

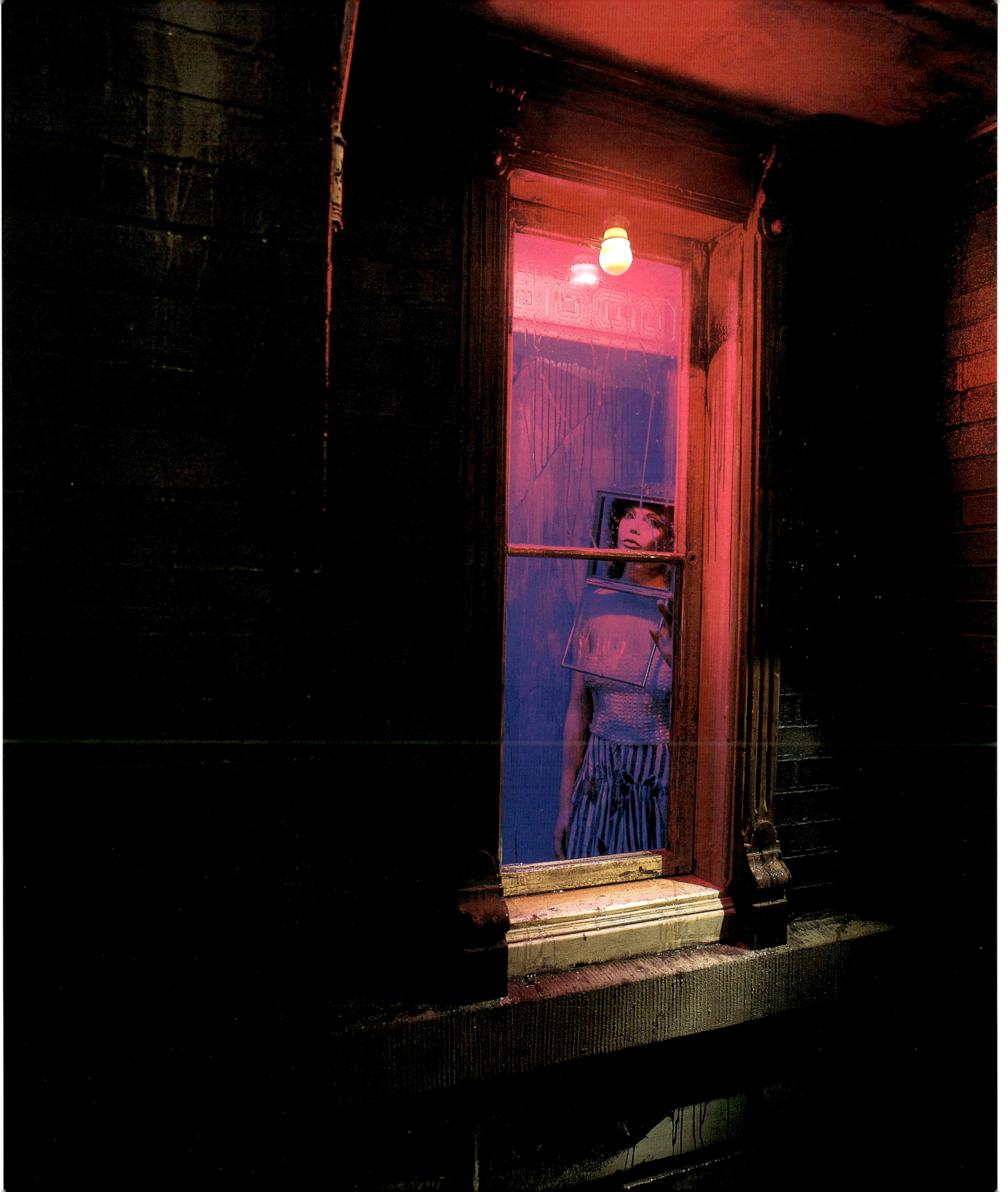

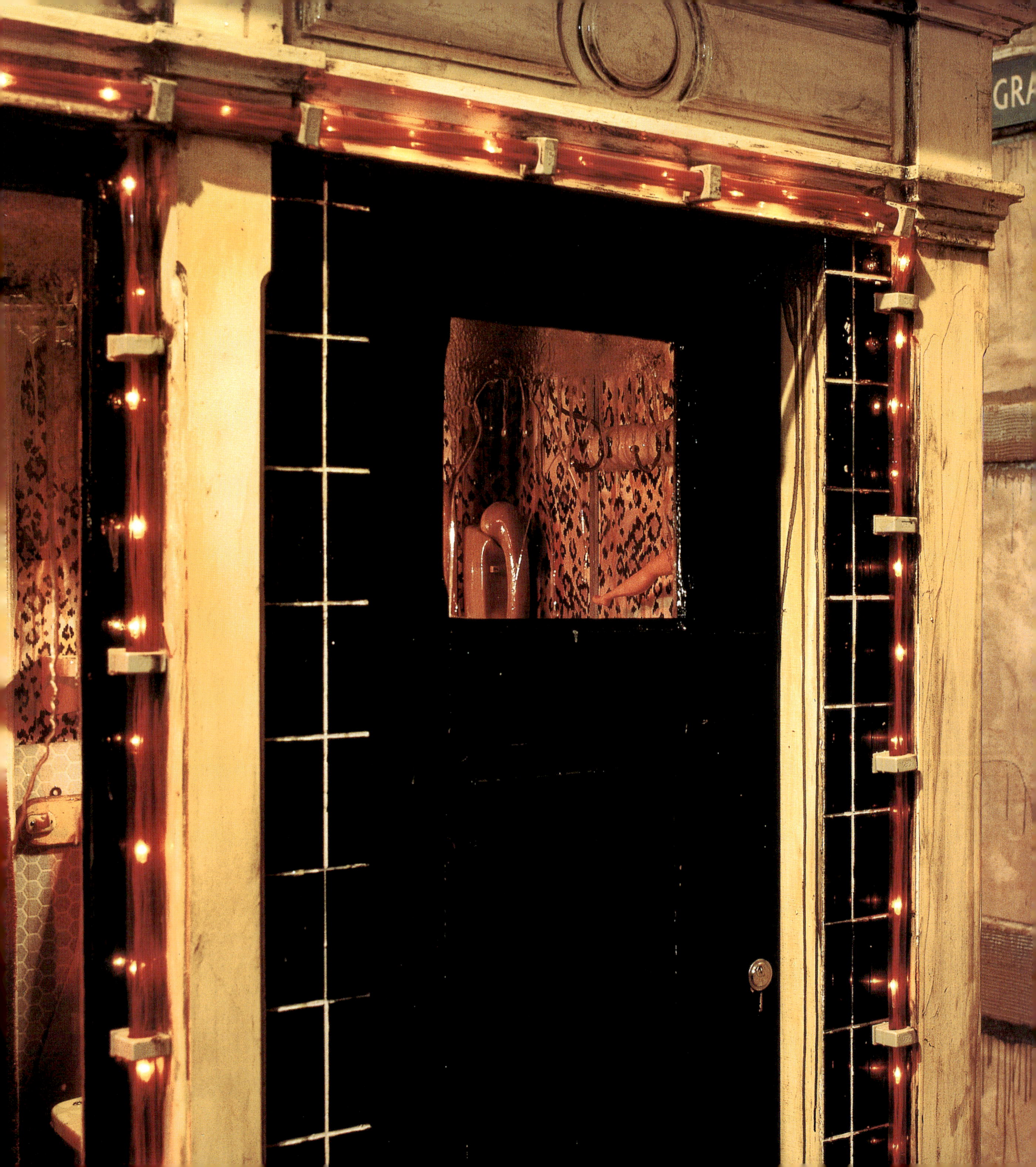

GRA

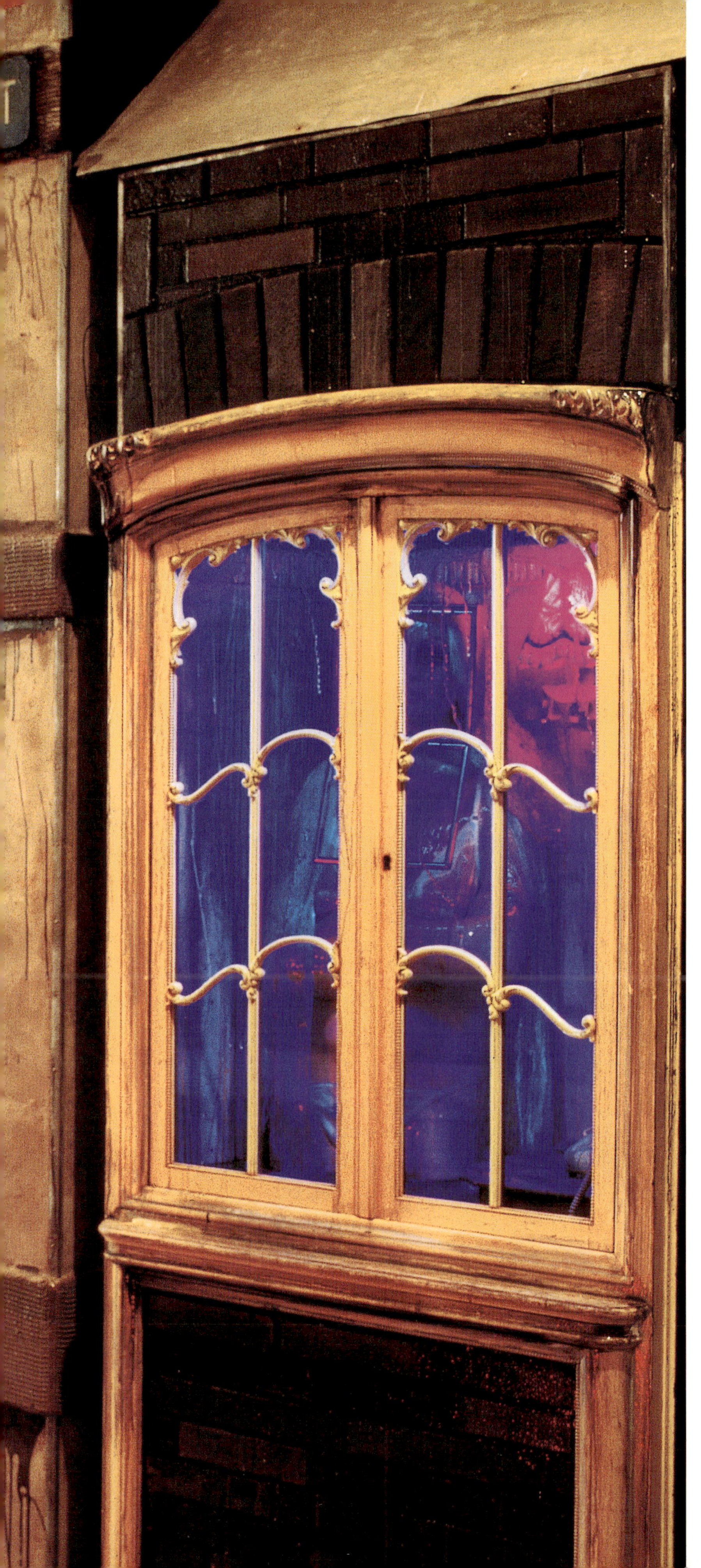

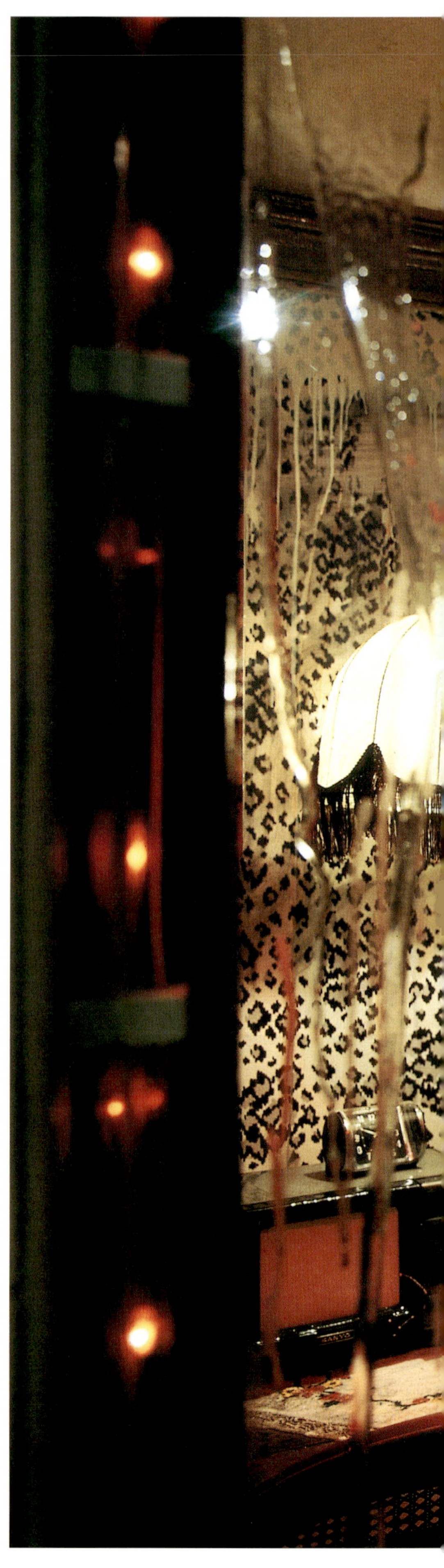

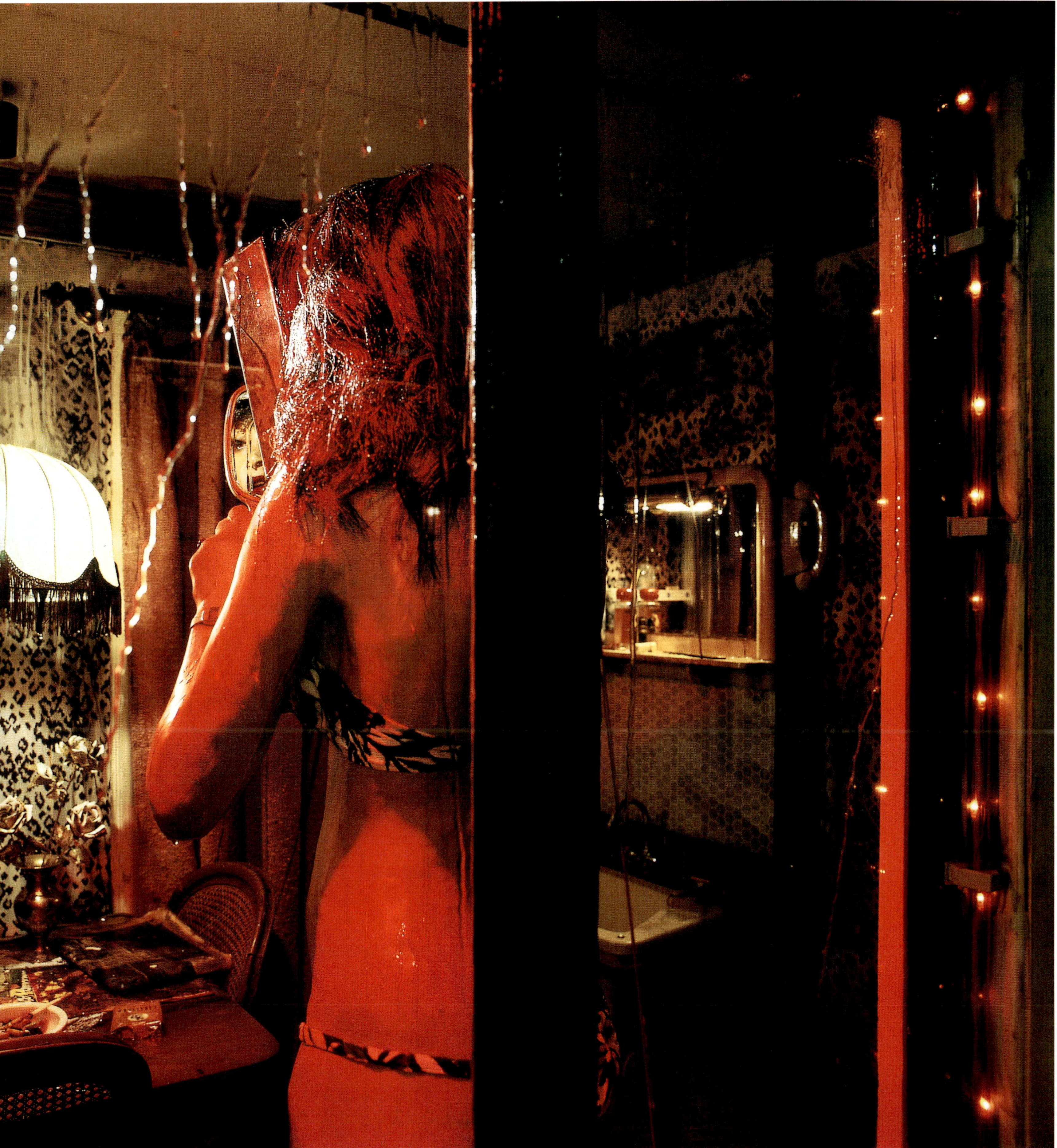

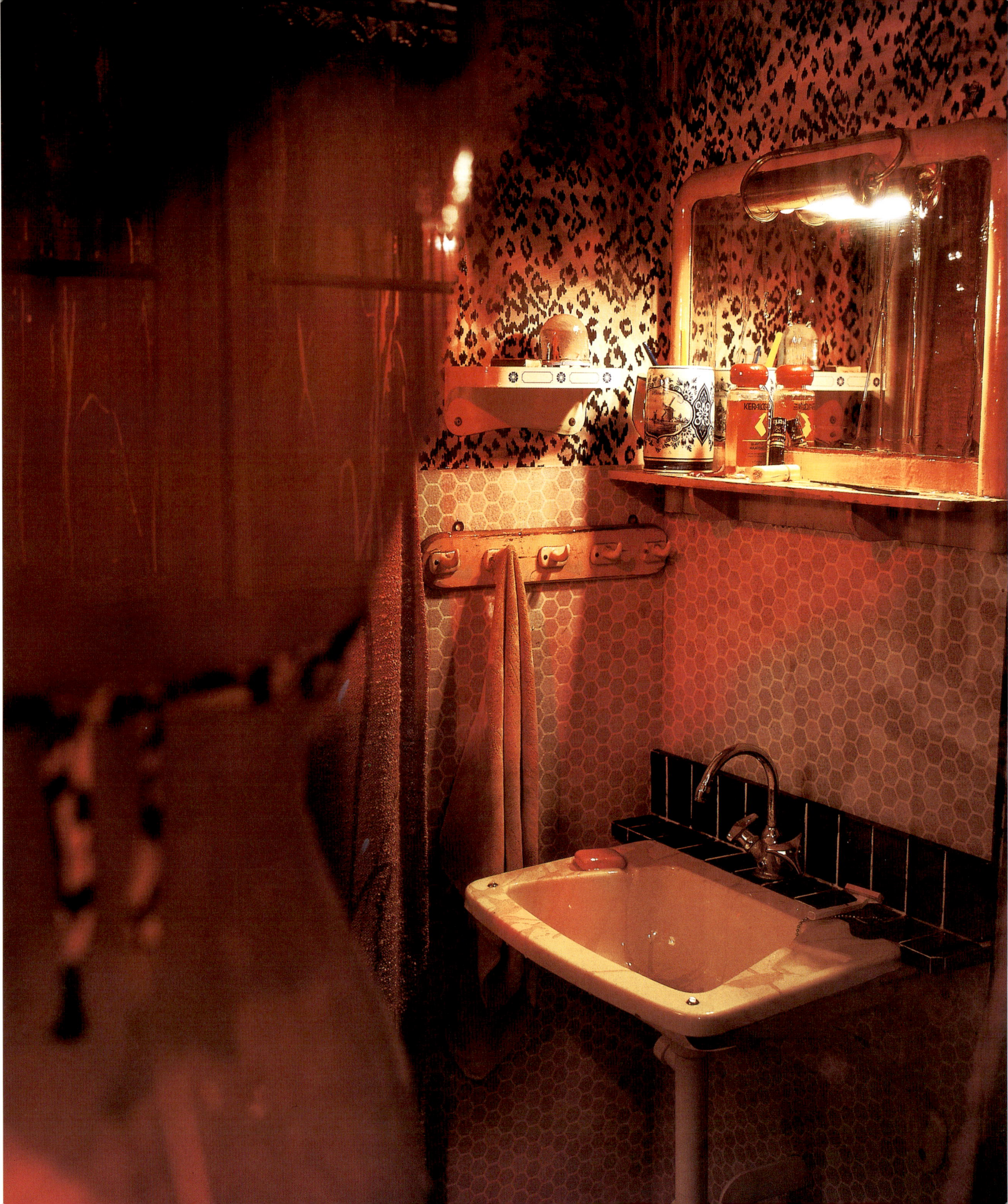

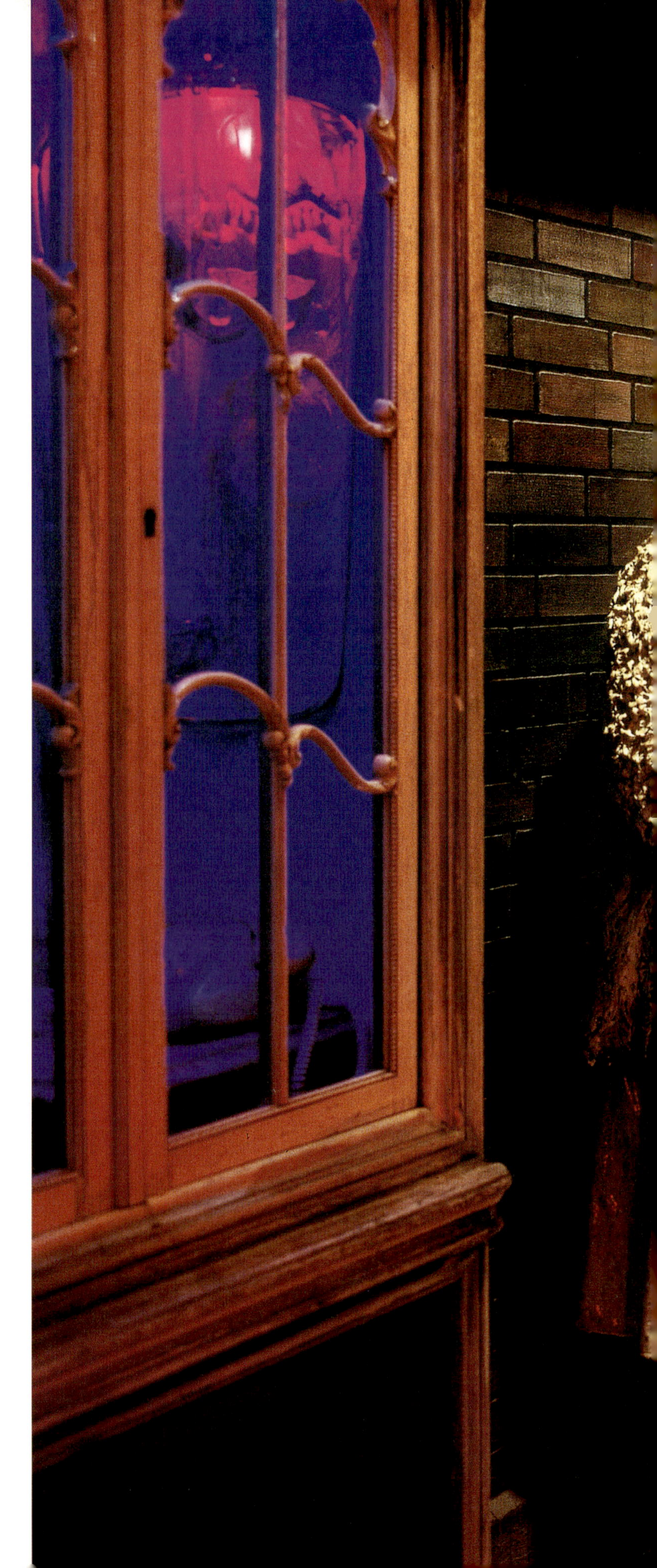

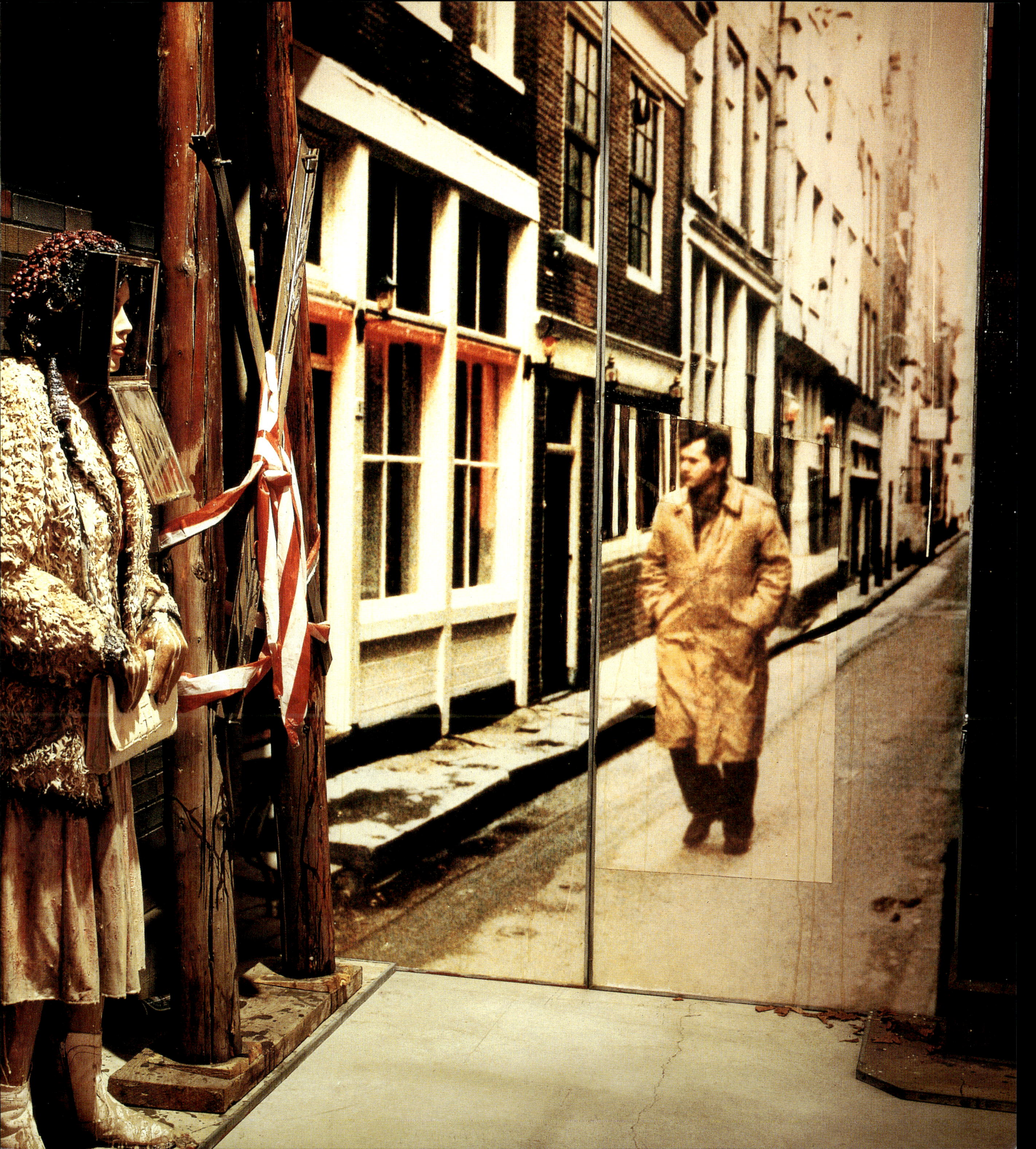

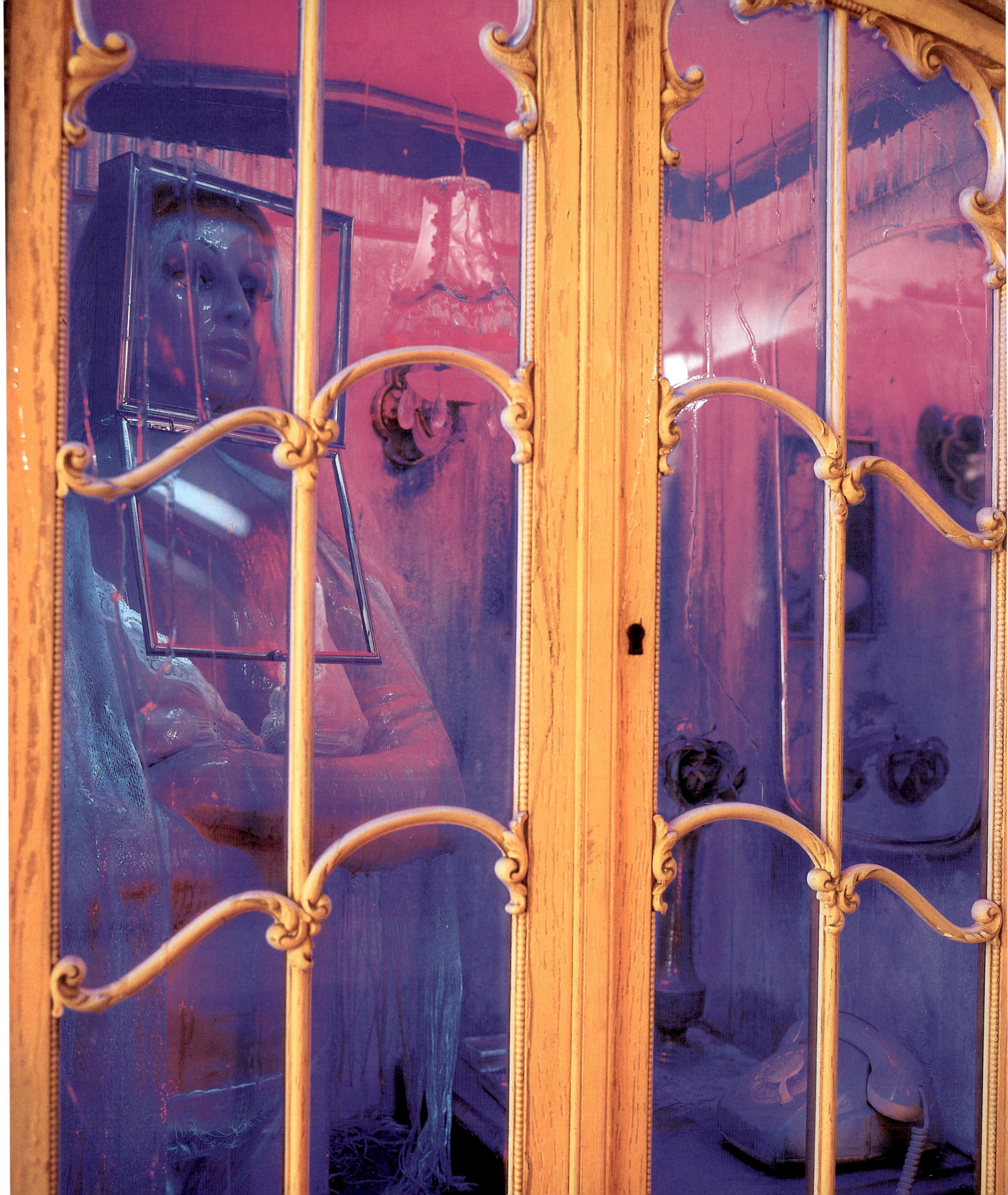

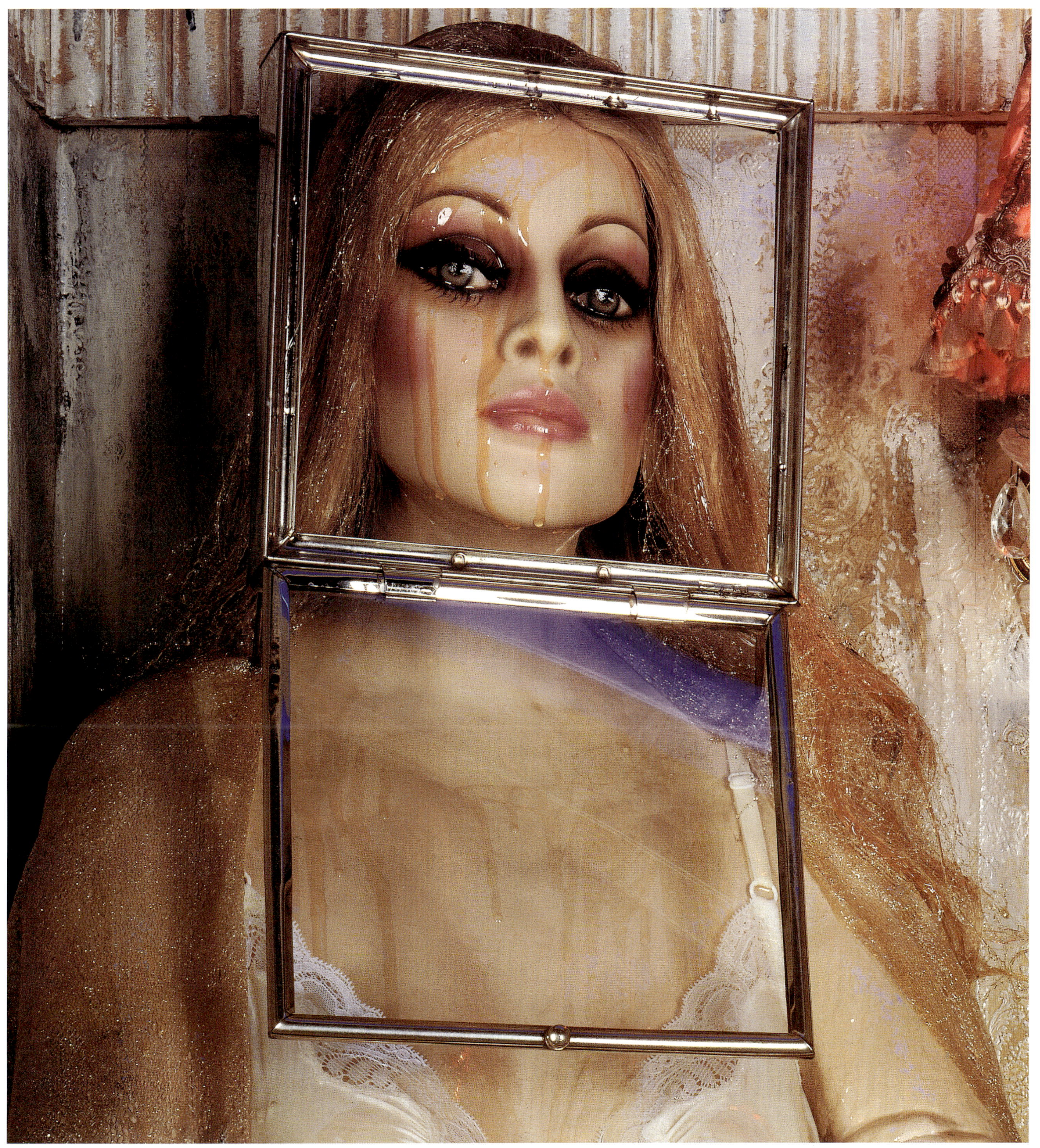

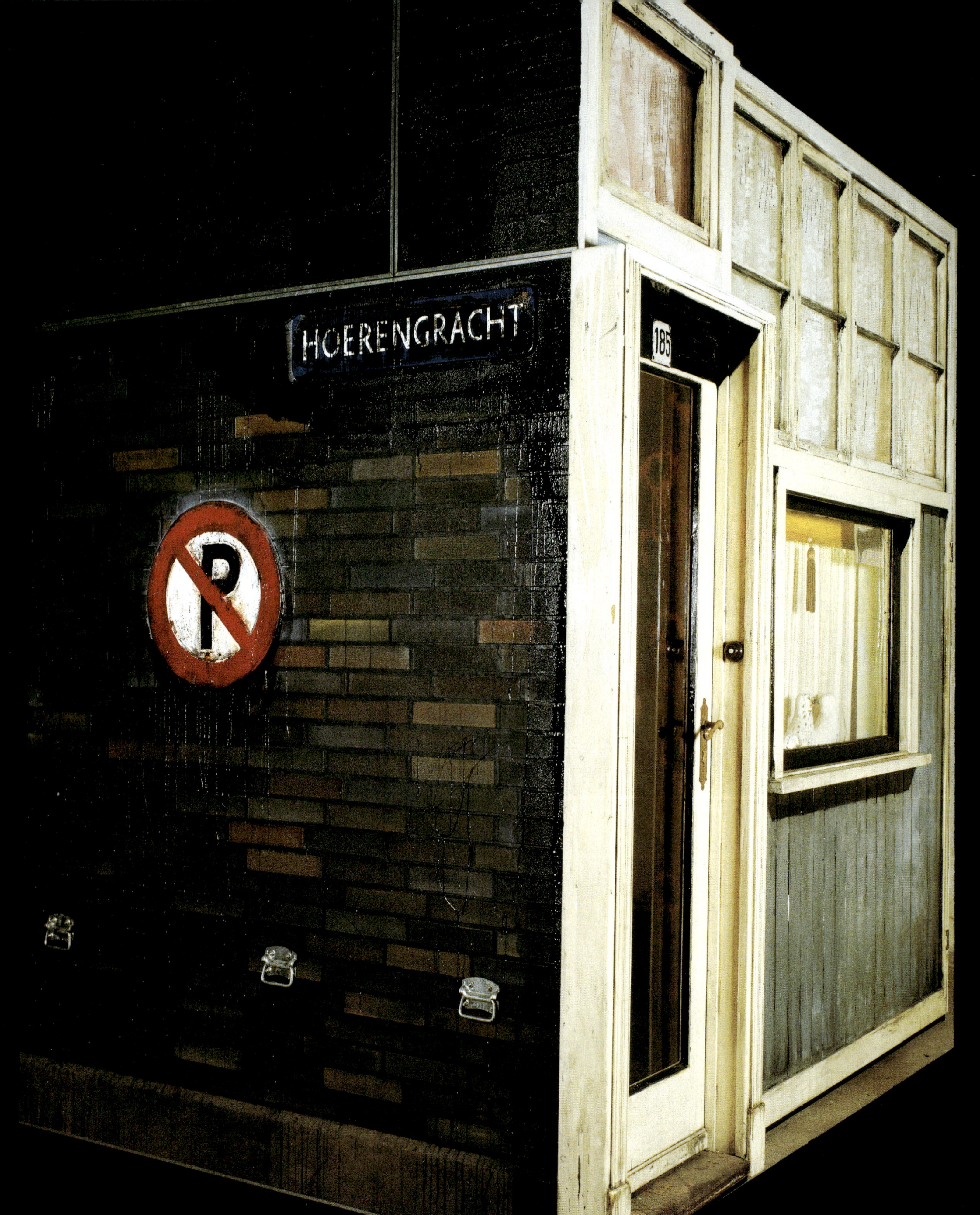
HOERENGRACHT
185
P

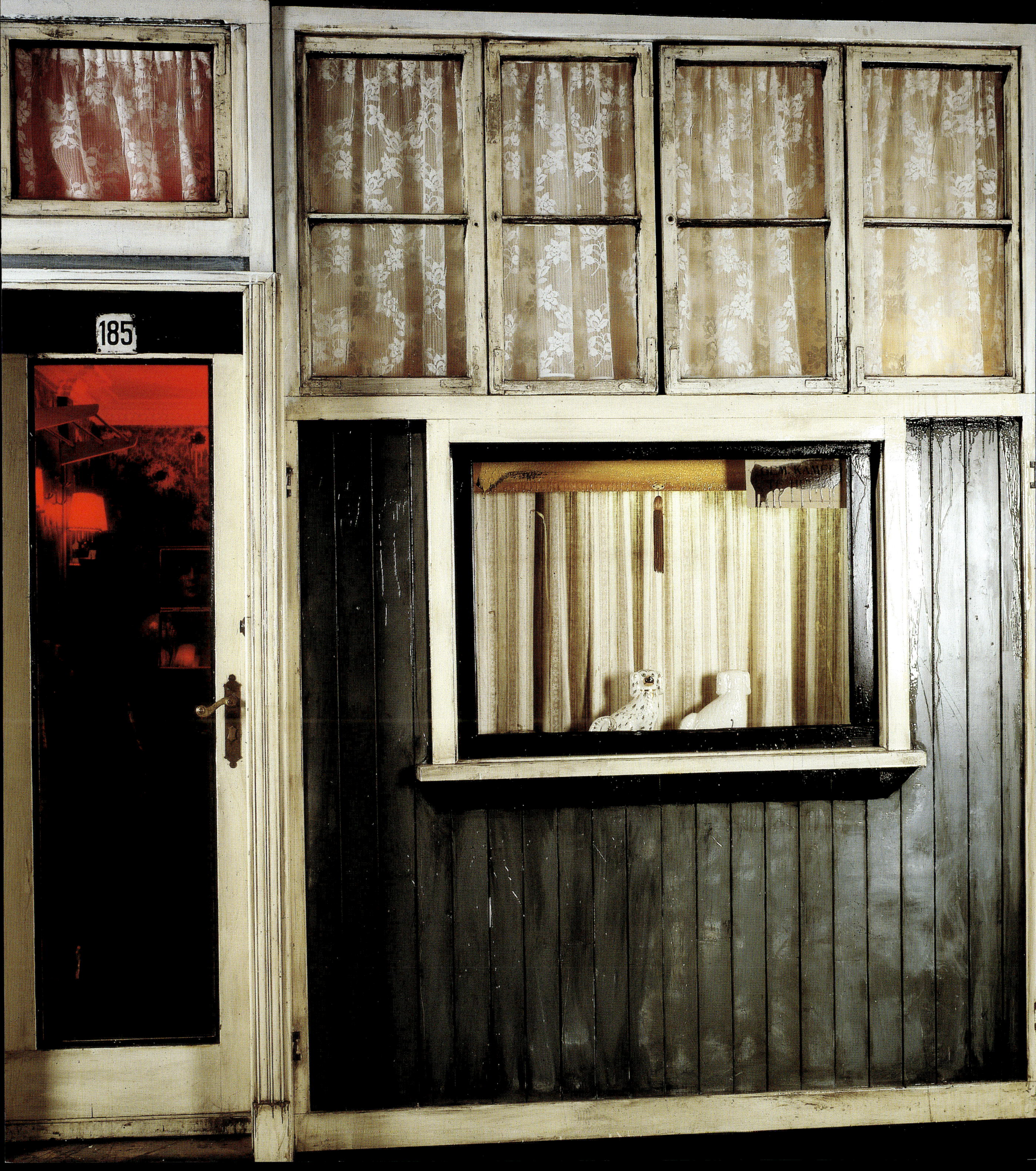

185

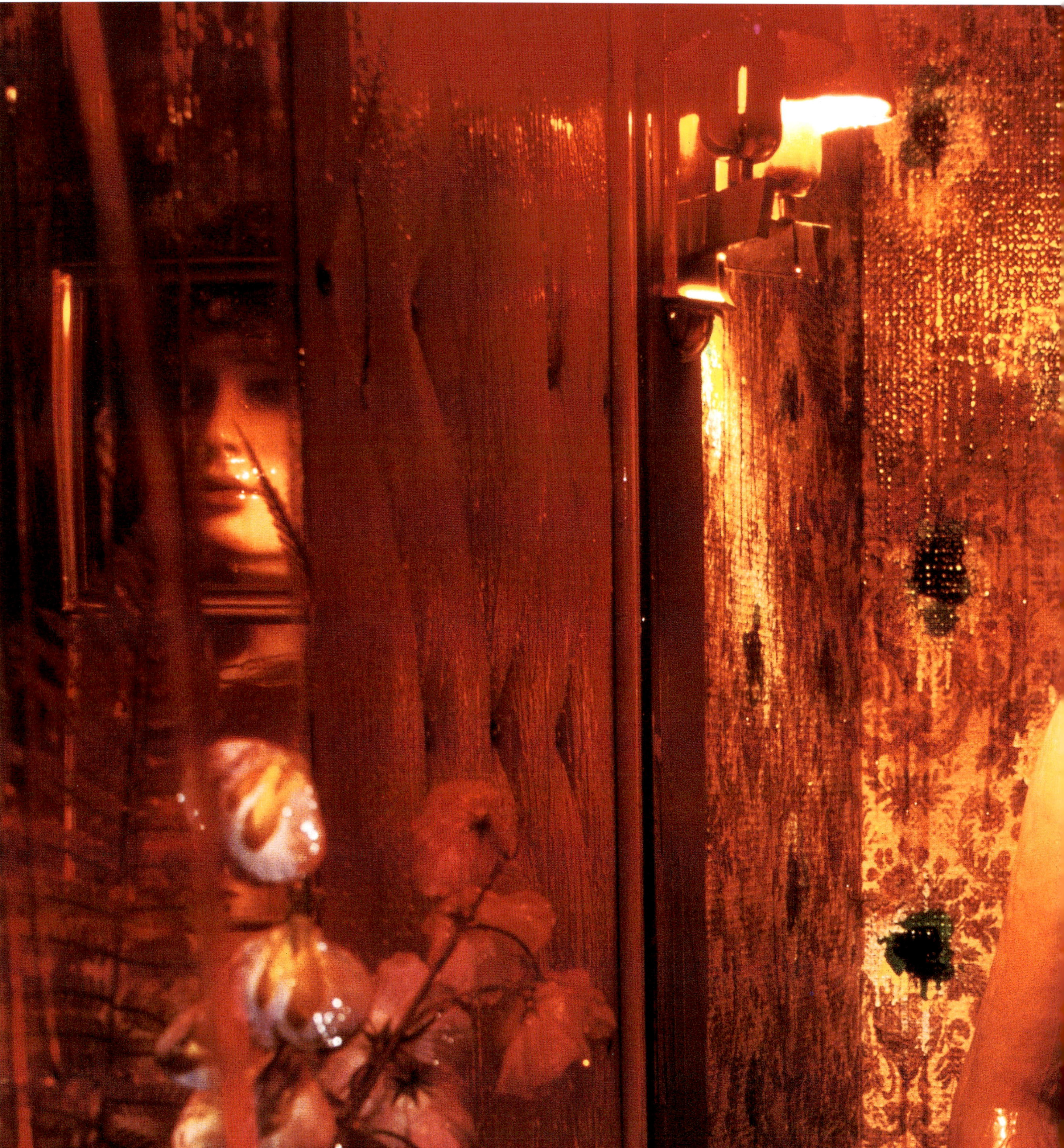

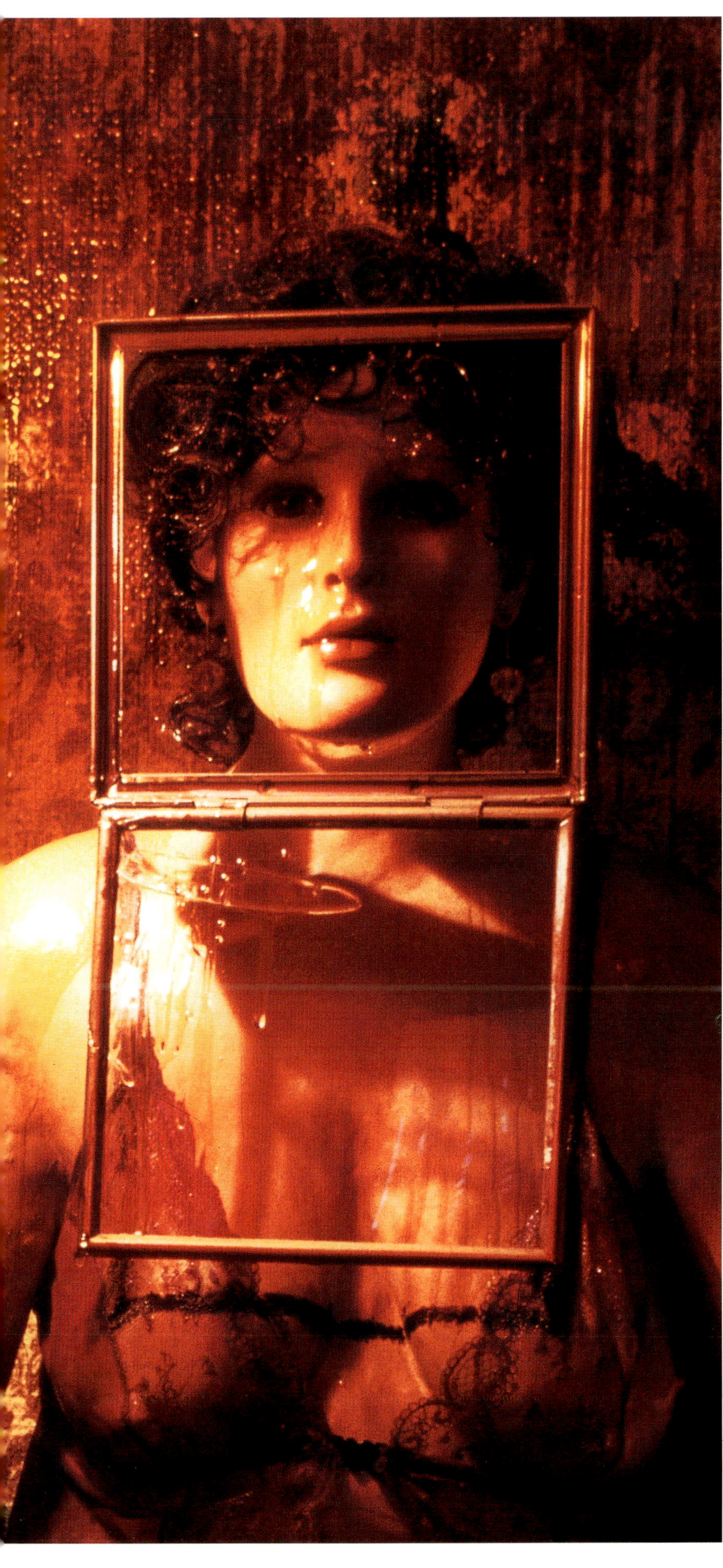

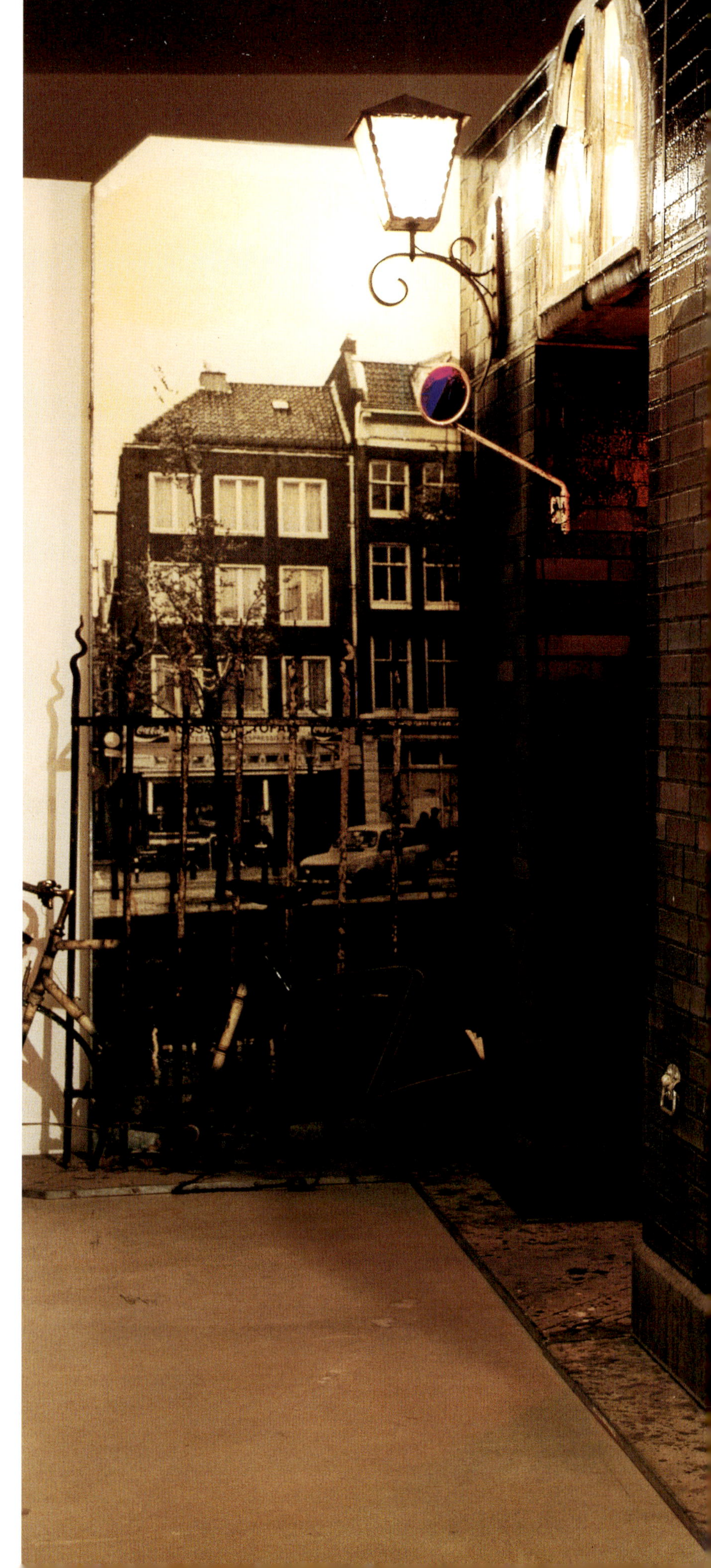

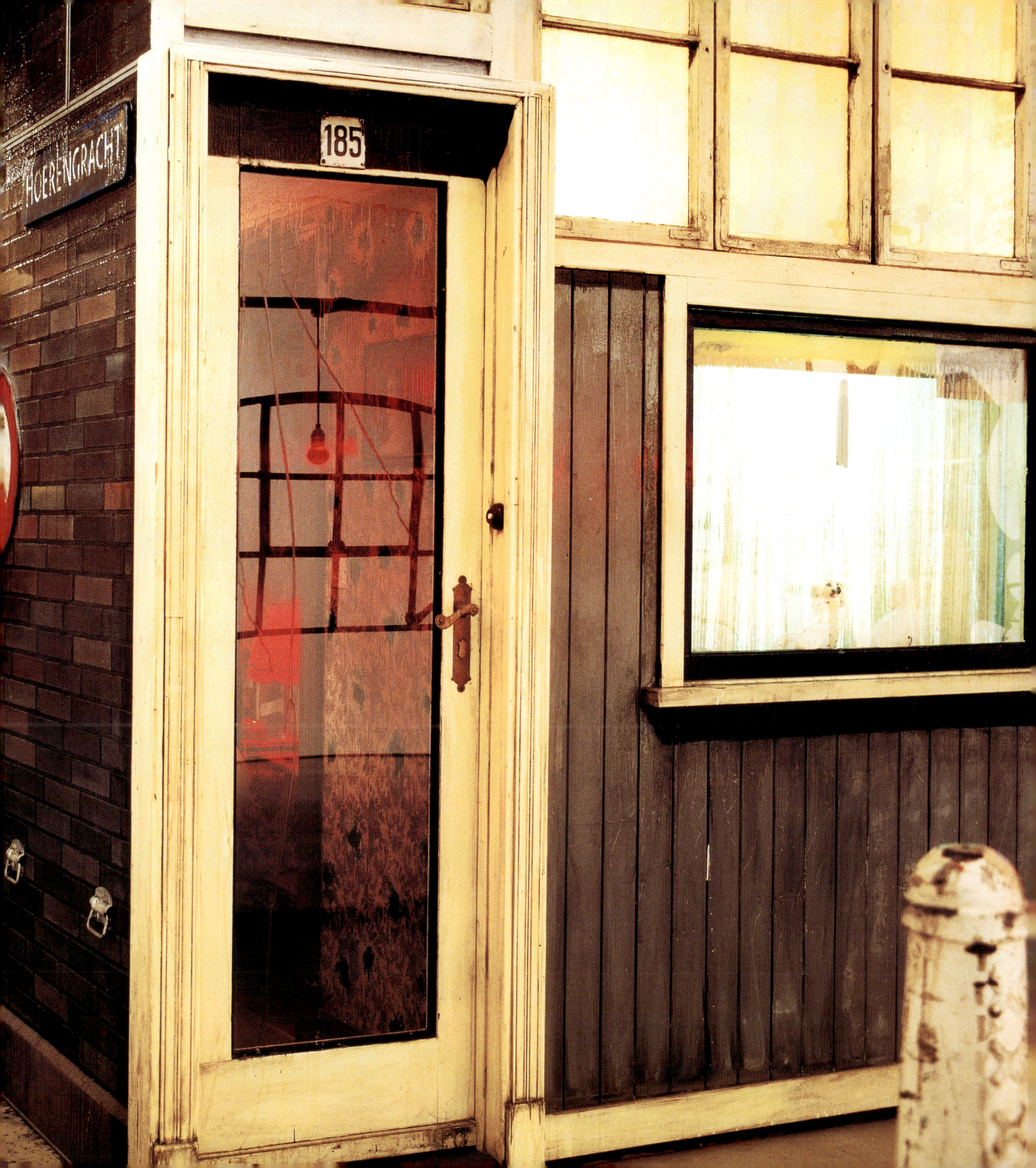

HOERENGRACHT
185

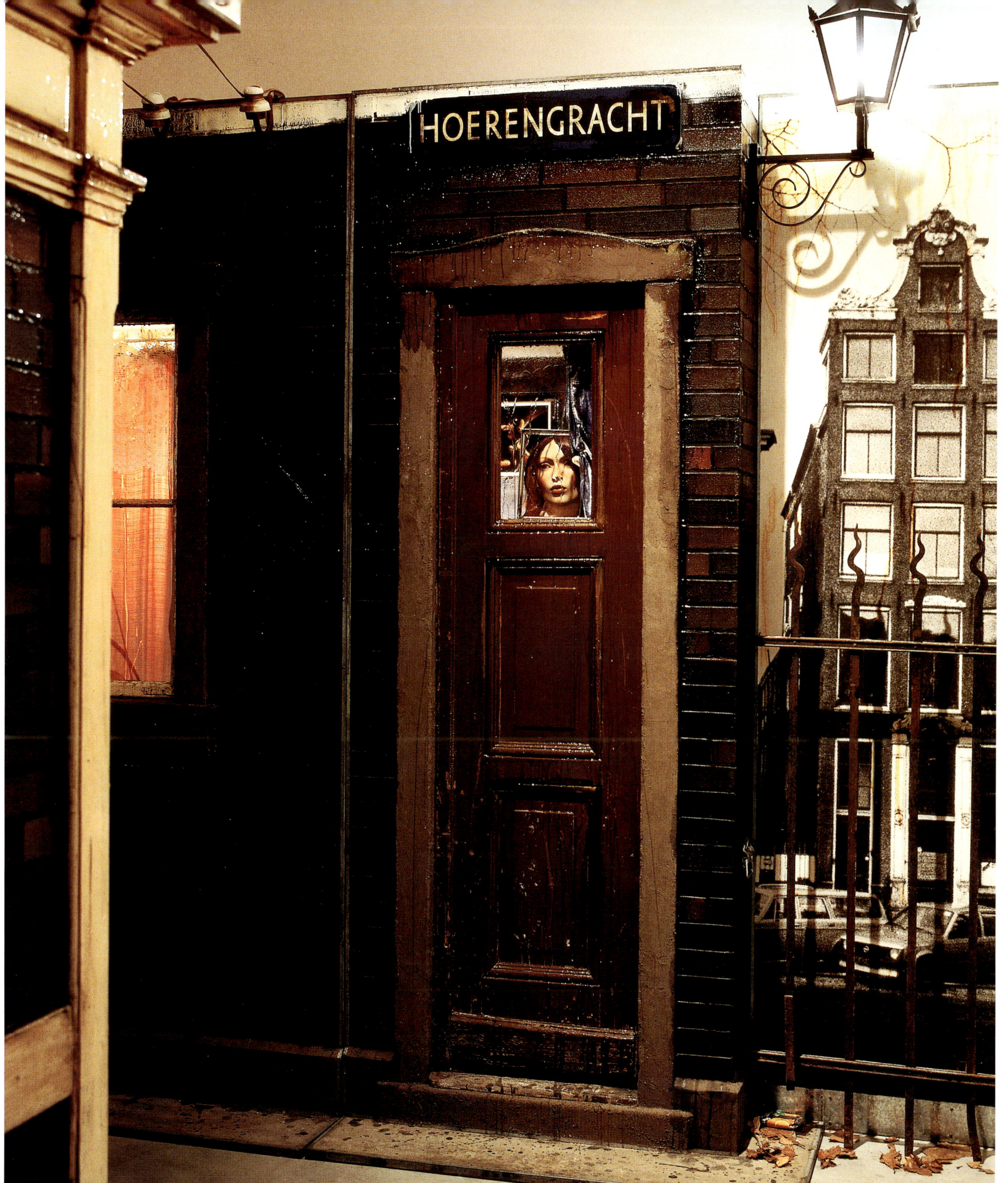
HOERENGRACHT

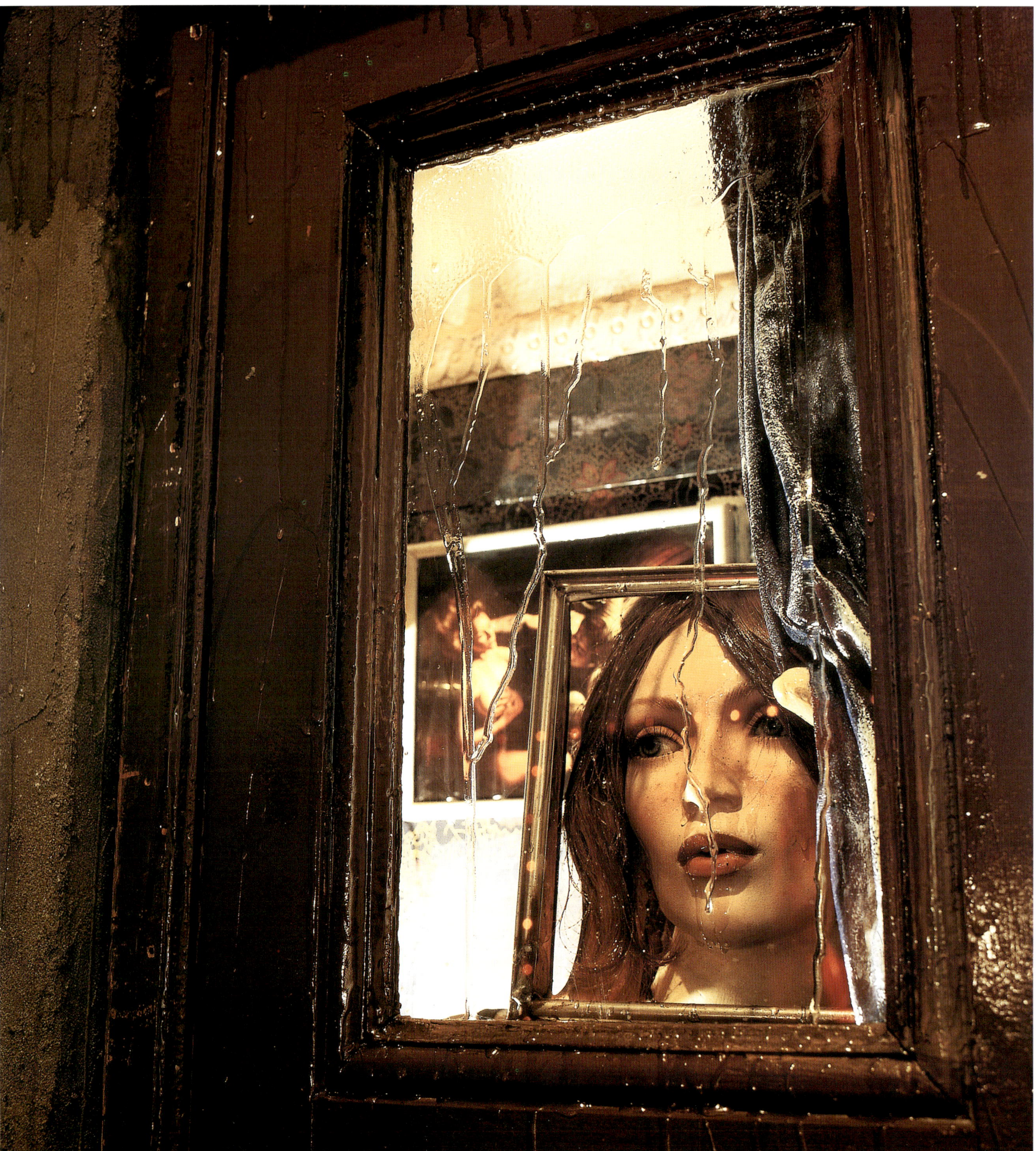

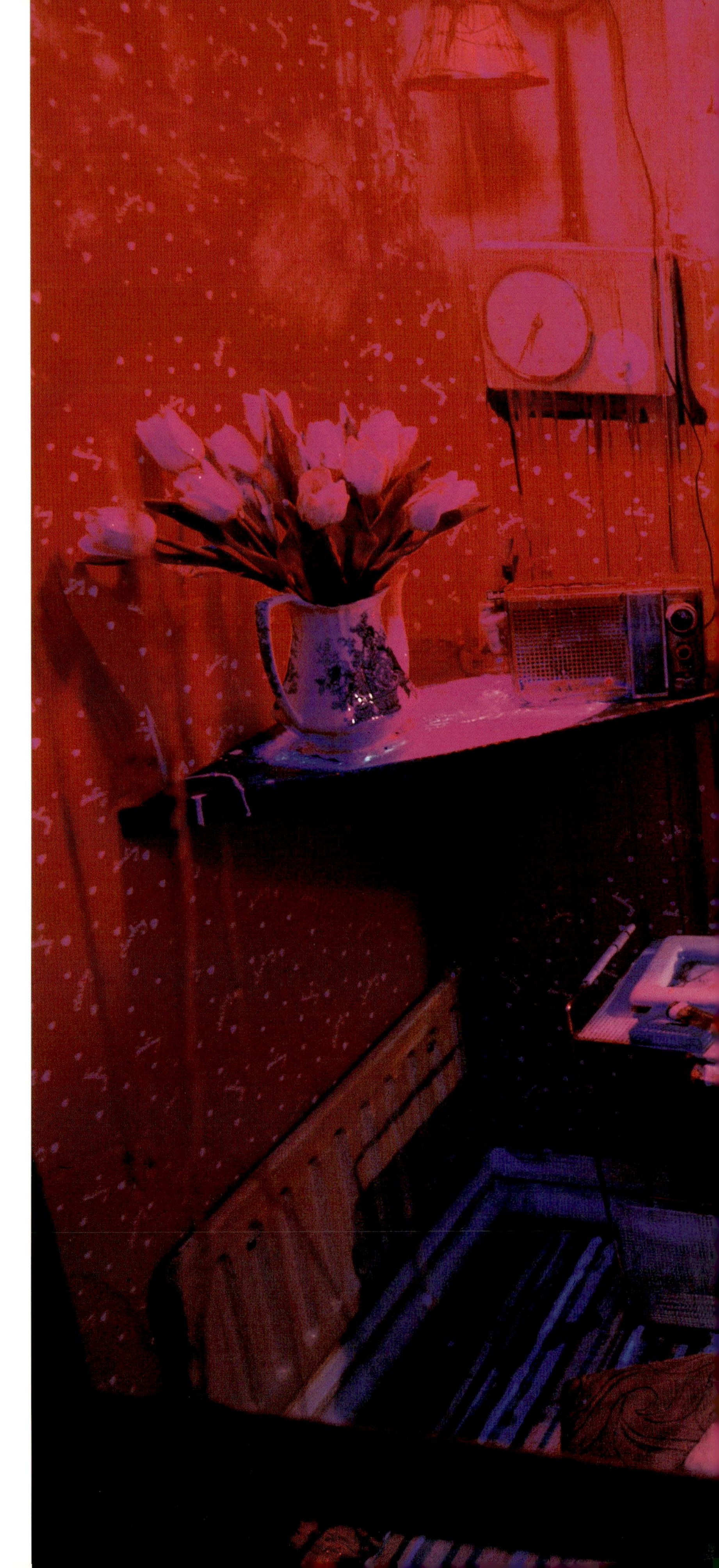

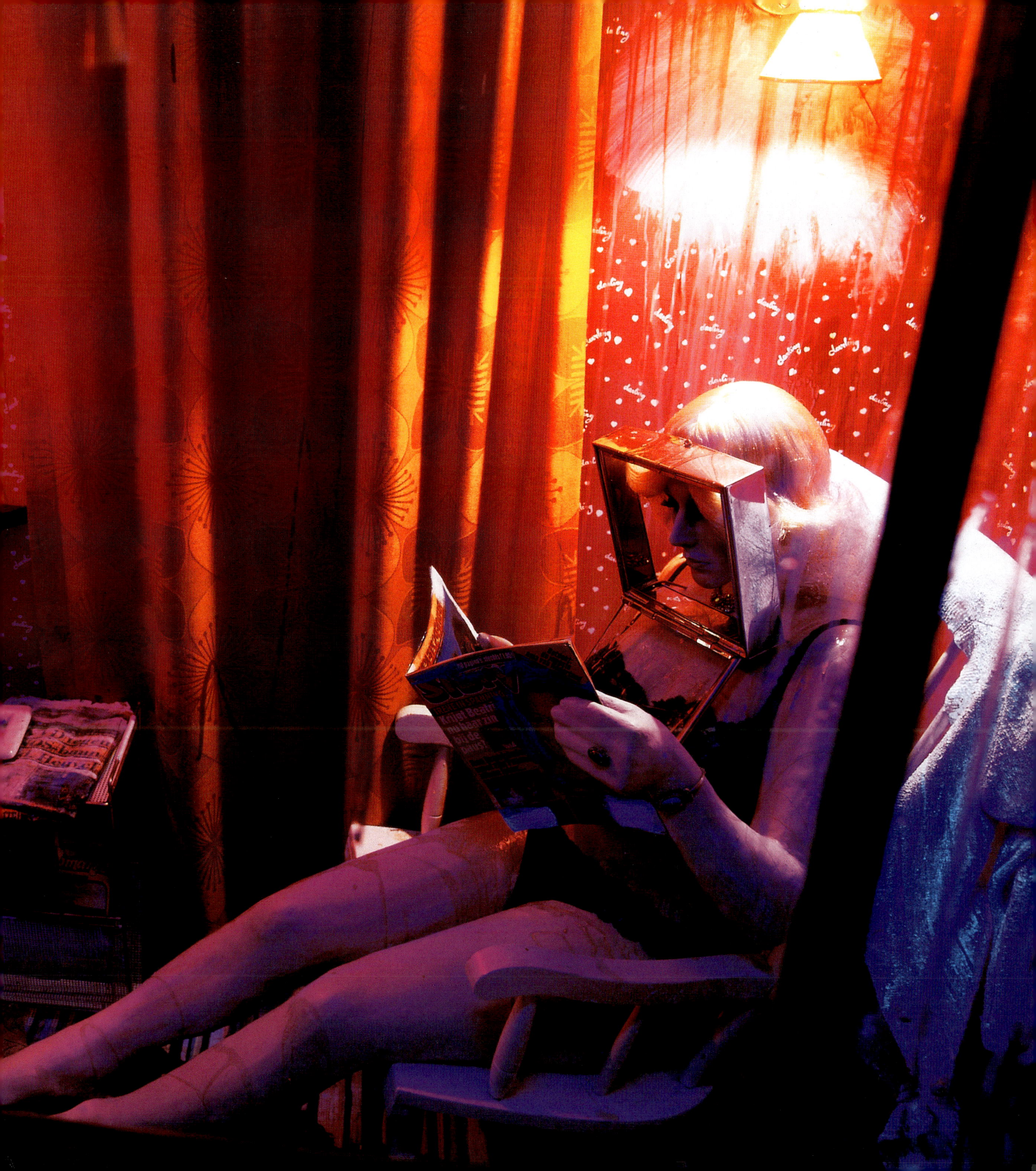

STORY
Krijgt Beatrix
na haar 37ste
op de
troon?

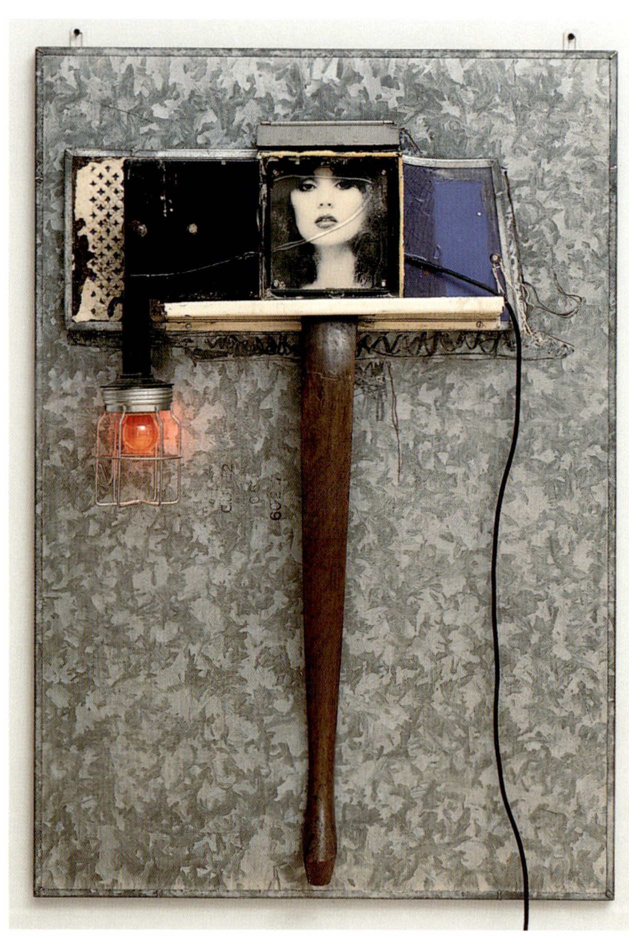

Drawing for The Hoerengracht No. 5
1985, mixed media
42 x 28 x 5"

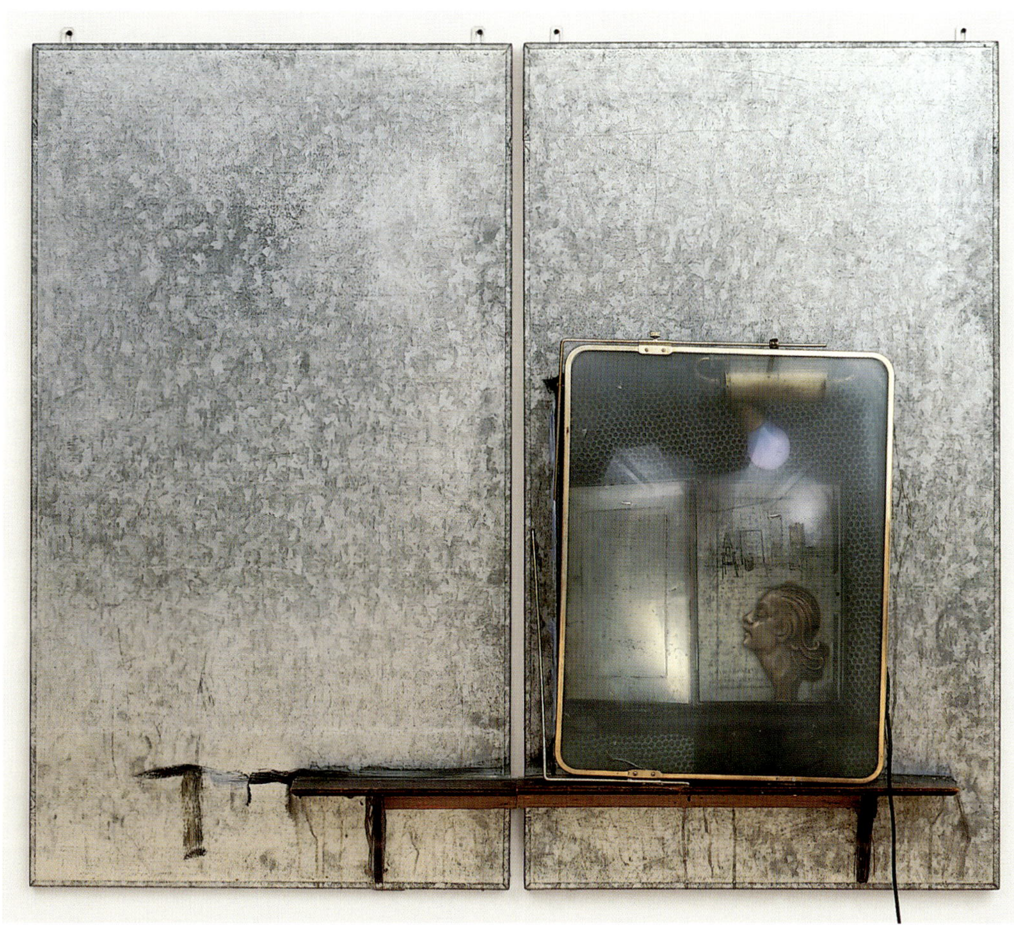

Drawing for The Hoerengracht No. 7
1985, mixed media
50½ x 60 x 5"

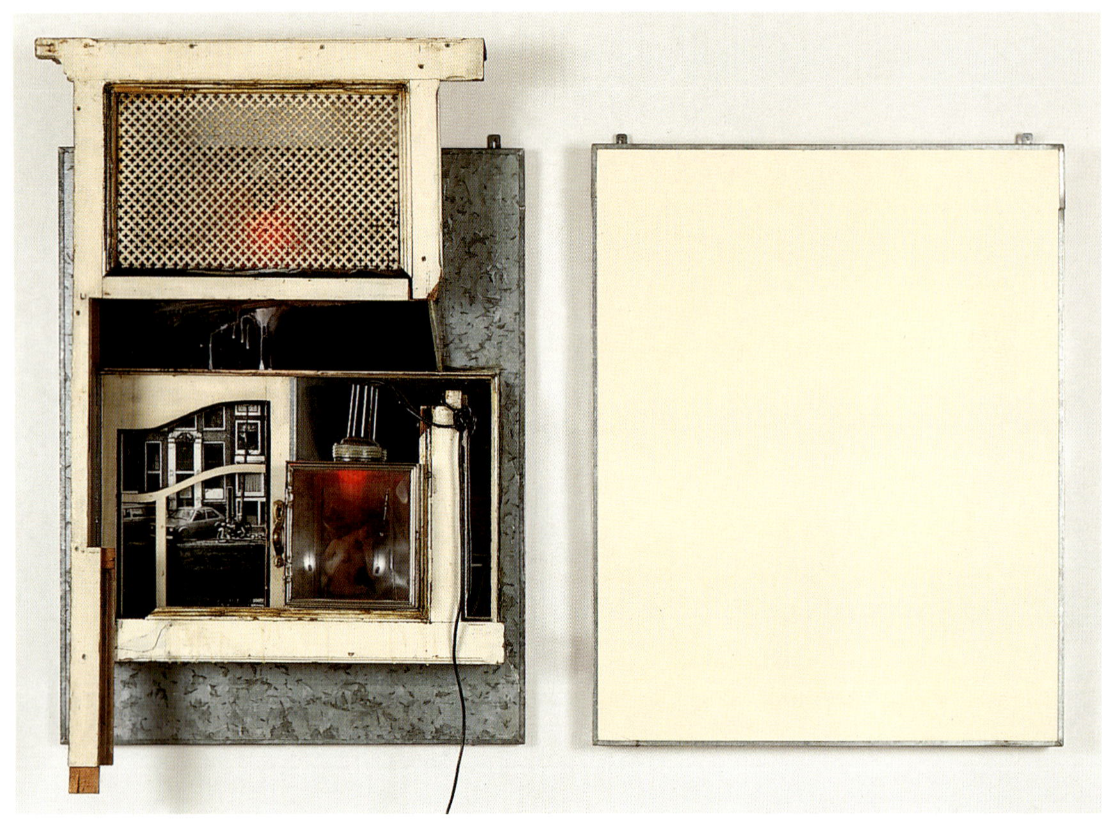

Drawing for The Hoerengracht No. 8
1985, mixed media
49 x 58½ x 6"

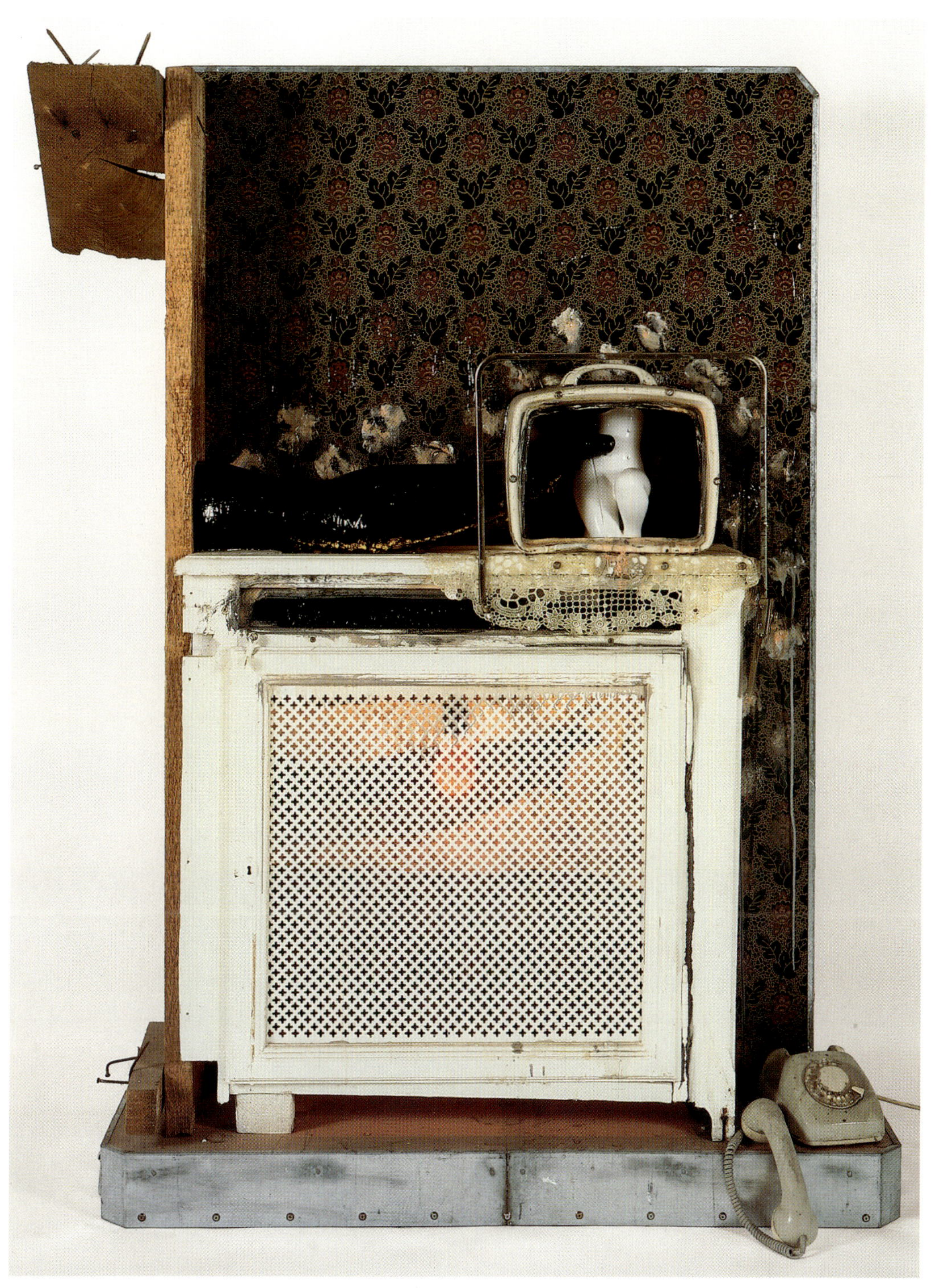

Drawing for The Hoerengracht No. 9
1986, mixed media
65 x 47 x 13"

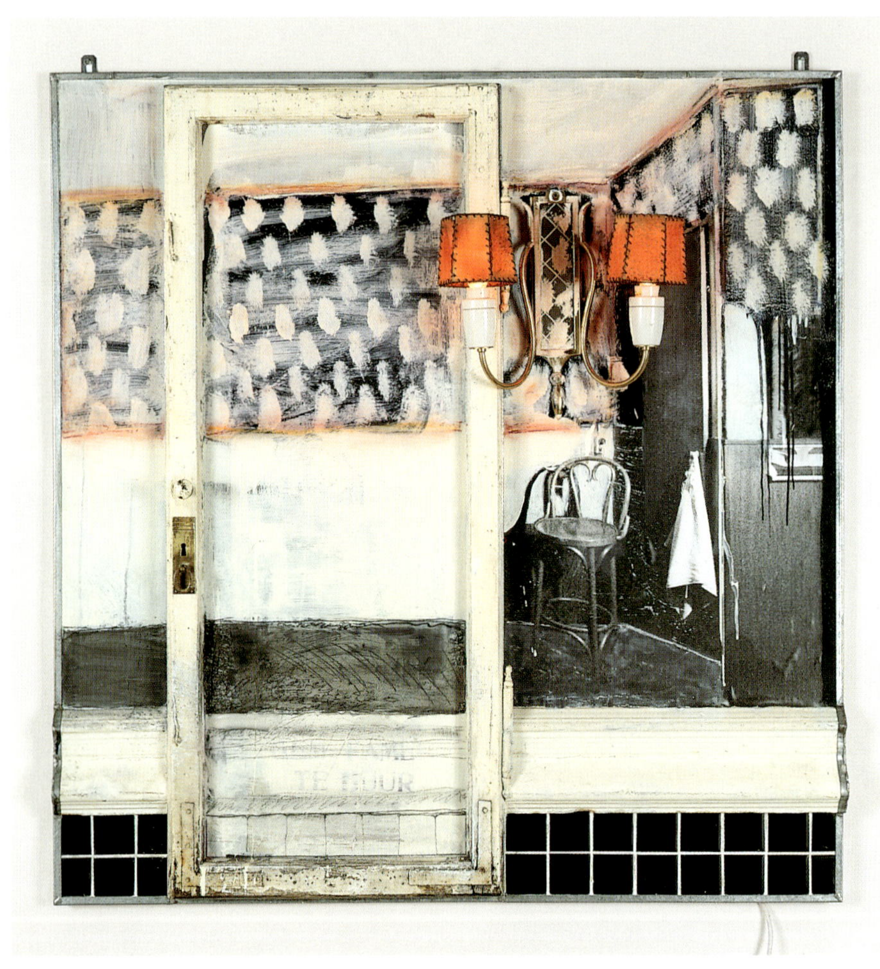

Drawing for The Hoerengracht No. 10
1987, mixed media
42 x 41 x 5"

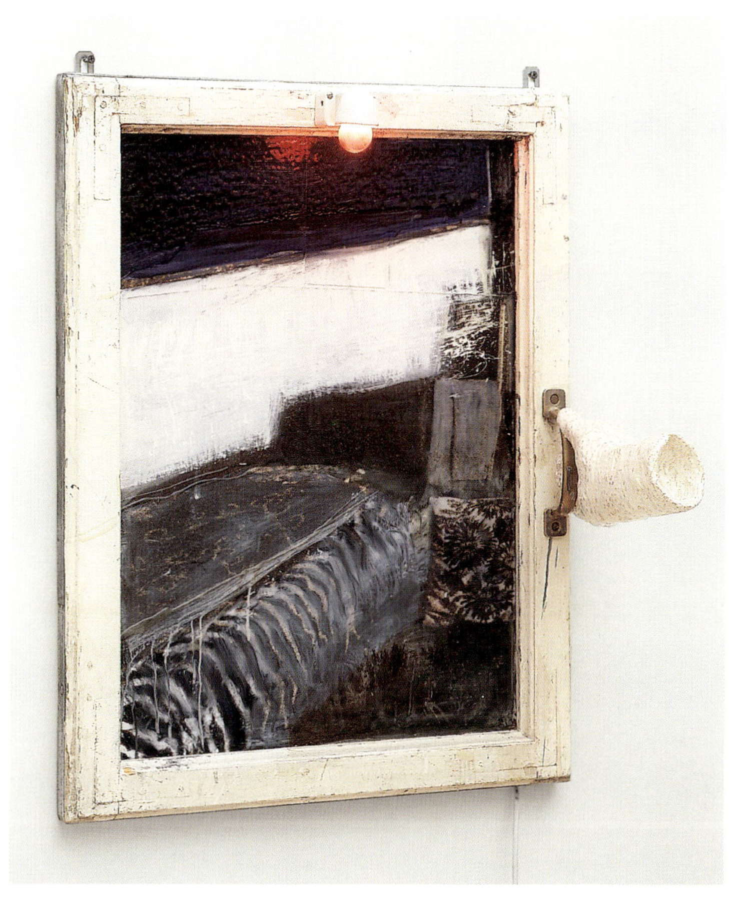

Drawing for The Hoerengracht No. 11
1987, mixed media
29 x 23 x 11"

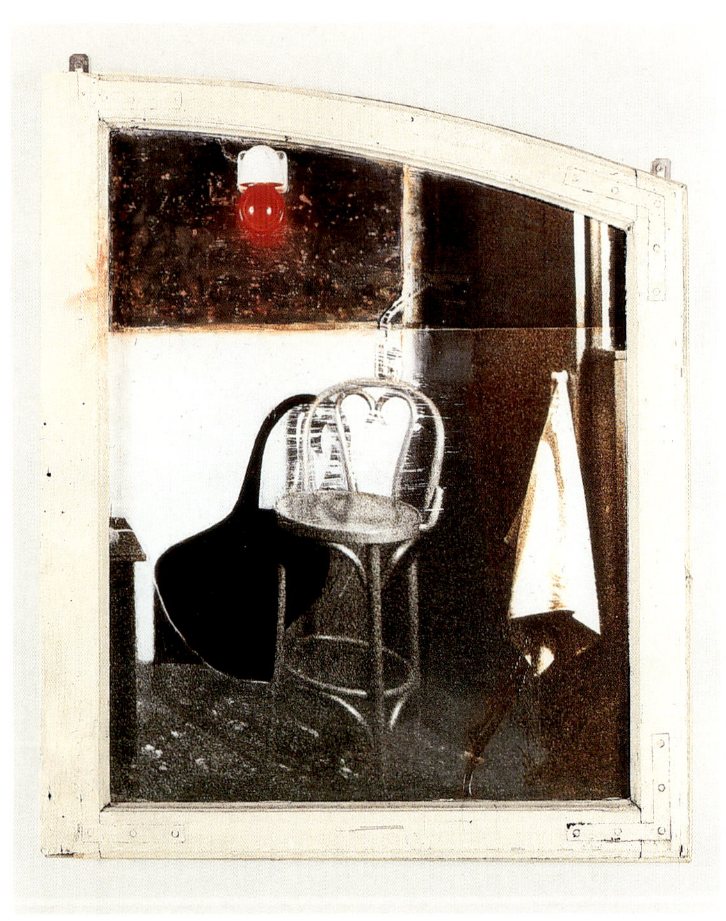

Drawing for The Hoerengracht No. 12
1987, mixed media
30 x 25 x 4"

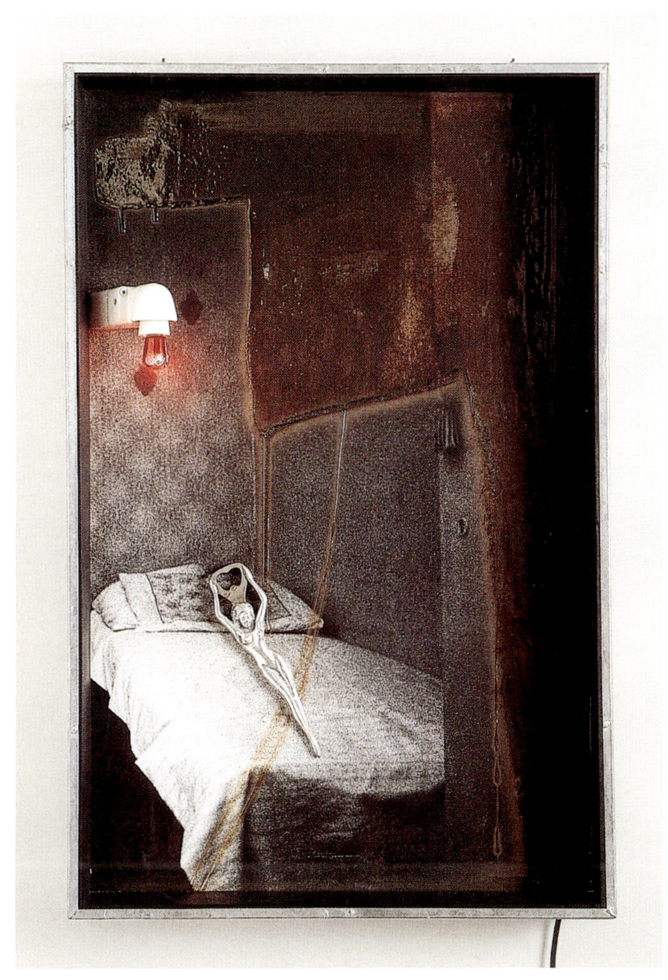

Drawing for The Hoerengracht No. 15
1987, mixed media
31¾ x 21½ x 4"

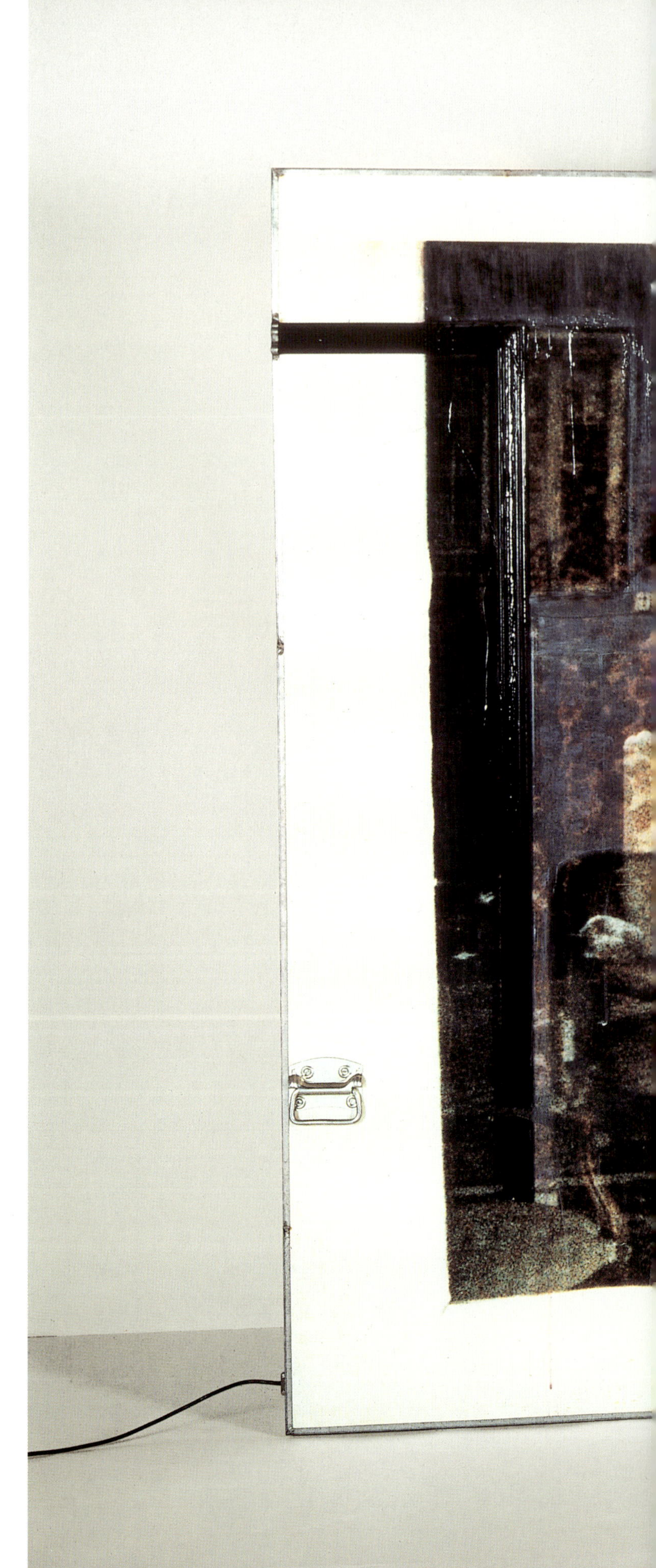

Woman Washing with Scrutator
1985, mixed media
81 x 98 x 27"

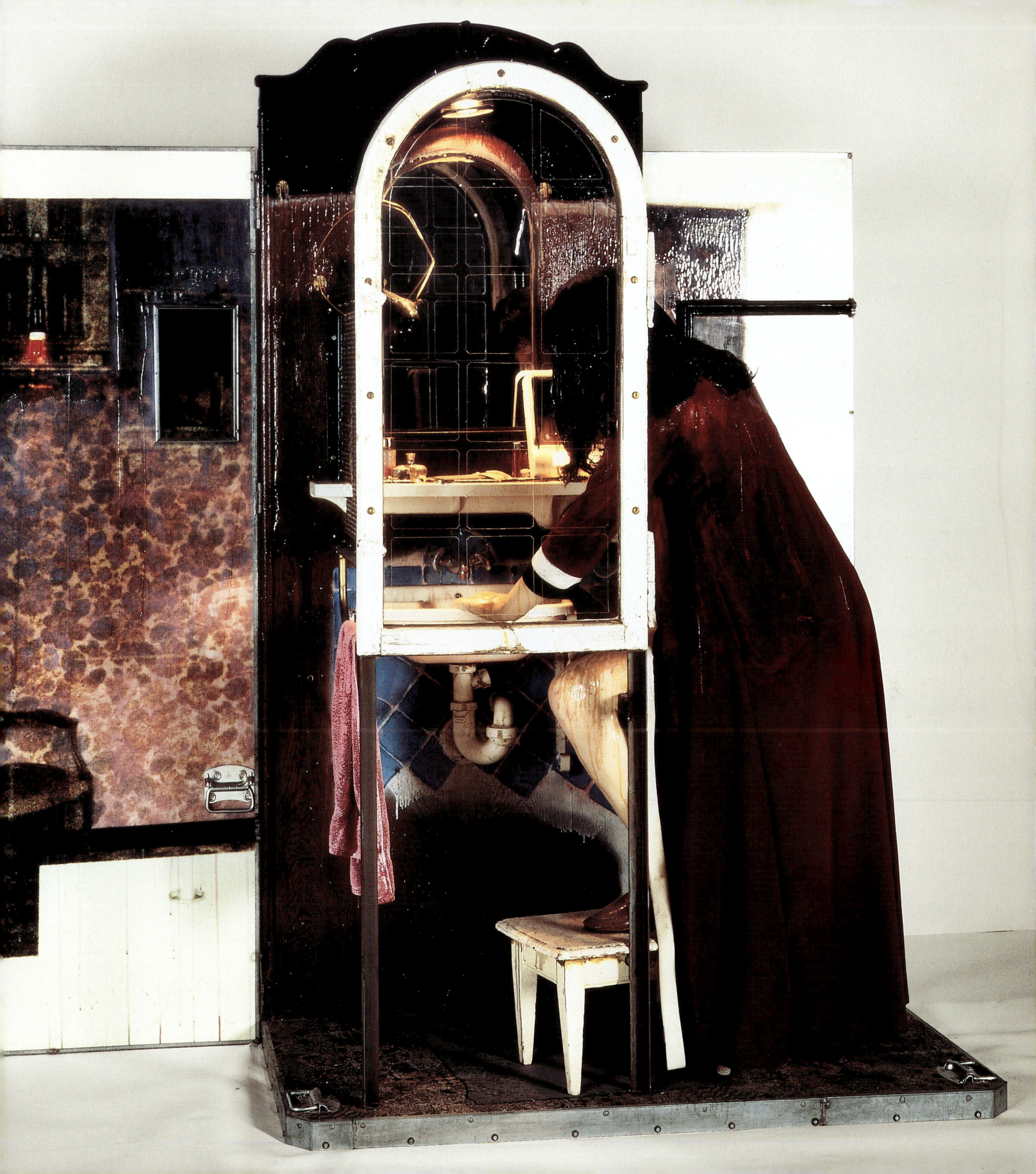

ED KIENHOLZ

| 1927 | Born in Fairfield, Washington |
| 1953-73 | Resident of Los Angeles |
| 1994 | Died in Hope, Idaho |

NANCY REDDIN KIENHOLZ

| 1943 | Born in Los Angeles |
| | Lives and works in Hope, Idaho; Houston and Berlin |

Exhibitions before 1972 are by Edward Kienholz. Exhibitions after 1972 are by Edward Kienholz and Nancy Reddin Kienholz.

## SOLO EXHIBITIONS

Exhibitions accompanied by a catalogue are indicated with an asterisk

**2002** *The Hoerengracht*, PaceWildenstein, New York.

**2001** *Kienholz Tableau Drawings*, LA Louver, Venice, California.

**2000** *Ed and Nancy Kienholz*, Galerie Forsblom, Helsinki.

**1996** *Kienholz: A Retrospective*, Whitney Museum, New York; Museum of Contemporary Art Los Angeles.

*The Merry-Go-World*, Kunsthalle Düsseldorf, Germany.

*The Merry-Go-World Or Begat By Chance And The Wonder Horse Trigger and Mono-Series*, Hugh Lane Municipal Gallery of Modern Art, Dublin.

**1995** *Edward Kienholz 1954-62*, The Menil Collection, Houston.

**1994** *76 J.C.s Led the Big Charade And Other Works*, L.A. Louver, Venice, California.

*The Merry-Go-World Or Begat By Chance And The Wonder Horse Trigger*, Spiral/Wacoal Art Center, Tokyo; Ashima City Museum, Ashima, Japan; Sonje Museum of Art, Seoul.

**1993** *The Hoerengracht*, Museum of Contemporary Art, San Diego.

**1992-93** Mono-series works from *The Merry-Go-World Or Begat By Chance And The Wonder Horse Trigger*, Galerie Redmann, Berlin; Betty Moody Gallery, Houston; and Braunstein/Quay Gallery, San Francisco.

*The Merry-Go-World Or Begat By Chance And The Wonder Horse Trigger*, L.A. Louver, Venice, California and Louver Gallery New York; Minneapolis Institute of Art; Museum of Fine Arts, Houston.

**1990** *Edward and Nancy Kienholz: 1980s*, Nishimura Gallery, Tokyo.

**1989** *Edward and Nancy Kienholz: 1980s*, Städtische Kunsthalle Düsseldorf; Museum Moderner Kunst, Vienna.

*Louver Gallery, New York.

Gemini G.E.L. Gallery, Los Angeles.

**1988** *The Caddy Court*, The Art Museum of Santa Cruz County, California; Memorial Union Art Gallery, University of California, Davis, California.

*Double Cross*, Gemini G.E.L. Gallery, Los Angeles.

*Television and Radio*, Zabriskie Gallery, New York.

**1987** *Red, White and Blue Series*, Braunstein/Quay Gallery, San Francisco.

*The Caddy Court*, L.A. Louver/Second Annual International Contemporary Art Fair, Los Angeles.

*Meiden-Macht-Maniupulation*, Kulturverein Zehntscheuer Rottenberg; Heidelberger Kunstverein, West Germany.

**1986** *Grey Works*, L.A. Louver Gallery, Venice, California.

*The Pedicord Apartments* and *Drawing for the Pedicord Apartments*, The American Center, Paris.

*Kienholz: The Ozymandias Parade*, Portland Center for the Visual Arts, Oregon.

*The Pawn Boys*, Berlinische Galerie, Berlin.

*The Art Show*, Santa Barbara Contemporary Arts Forum.

*Sollie 17*, The Detroit Institute of Arts.

1985    The Chicago *Art Show*, Museum of Contemporary Art, Chicago.

1984    *Human Scale*, San Francisco Museum of Modern Art; Contemporary Arts Museum, Houston; Walker Art Center, Minneapolis; Museum of Contemporary Art, Chicago.

*The Art Show*, Braunstein Gallery, San Francisco.

*Kienholz in Context*, Cheney Cowles Memorial Museum, Eastern Washington State Historical Society, and Touchstone Center for the Visual Arts, Spokane.

*Arbeiten von 1957-1963*, Reinhard Onnasch Galerie, Berlin.

1983    Brunswick Gallery, Missoula, Montana.

*The Kienholz Women*, Galerie Maeght, Paris.

*The Berlin Fountain*, Berlin Technischen Universität.

1982    *The Berlin Women*, Dibbert Gallery, Berlin.

*Still Live-1974 Installation*, Braunstein Gallery, San Francisco.

*Sollie 17*, Newport Harbor Art Museum, California.

*Sollie 17* and *Tableaux*, The Contemporary Arts Center, Cincinnati.

*Roxys and Other Works from the Reinhard Onnasch Collection*, Gesellschaft für Aktuelle Kunst, Bremen, West Germany.

1981    *The Kienholz Women*, Galerie Maeght, Zurich.

L.A. Louver Gallery, Venice, California.

*Tableaux 1961-1979*, The Douglas Hyde Gallery, Trinity College, Dublin.

*The White Easel Series*, Middendorf/Lane Gallery, Washington, D.C.

1980    Gemini G.E.L., Los Angeles.

1979    Udigvet af Louisiana Humlebaek, Denmark.

*The Volksempfängers*, Mannheim Kunstverein, West Germany; Galerie Maeght, Paris.

*Sculpture 1976-79*, Henry Art Gallery, University of Washington, Seattle.

University Art Gallery, University of Idaho, Moscow, Idaho.

*The Back Seat Dodge '38*, University Art Museum, University of California, Berkeley.

1978    *The Art Show*, Akademie der Kunst, Berlin.

1977    *The Art Show 1963-77*, Berliner Künstlerprogramm / DAAD; Galerie Folker Skulima, Berlin; Museé Nationale d'Art Moderne, Centre Georges Pompidou, Paris.

*The Volksempfängers*, The Nationalgalerie, Berlin; Bavarian National Gallery, Munich.

1975    *Roxys*, Museé da la Ville, Strasbourg.

Galerie Christel, Helsinki.

1974    Galleria Giancarlo Bocchi, Milan; Gallery LPS, Turino.

*The Eleventh Hour Final* and *The Tadpole Piano Pool with Woman Affixed Also*, Gallery Christel, Helsinki.

*Still Live*, Hochschule für bildende Kunst, Berlin, anläßlich der ADA 2, Berlin, ARS '74.

1973    Städtische Kunsthalle, Düsseldorf.

*Five Card Stud*, Berliner Künstlerprogramm / DAAD, Akademie der Kunst, Berlin.

Galerie Michael Werner, Cologne.

1972    Gemini G.E.L., Los Angeles.

Pasadena Art Museum.

Galerie Onnasch, Cologne.

Akademie der Kunst, Berlin.

1971    Kunsthaus, Zürich.

*Ten Tableaux*, Institute of Contemporary Art, London.

*Seven Works by Edward Kienholz*, Wide White Space Gallery, Antwerp.

1970    *11 & 11 Tableaux*, Moderna Museet, Stockholm.

*Watercolors*, Wide White Space, Antwerp, Galleria Francoise Lambert, Milan; Galerie Yvon Lambert, Paris.

*Dix Tableaux*, Centre National d'Art Contemporaine and Musée d'Art Moderne de la Ville de Paris.

*Kienholz: 1960-1970*, Städtische Kunsthalle, Düsseldorf.

1969    Ateneumin Taidemuseo, Helsinki.

*Watercolors*, Eugenia Butler Gallery, Antwerp.

1968    *The Eleventh Hour Final*, Gallery 669, Los Angeles.

Boise Gallery of Art, Idaho.

1967    *Work from the 1960s*, Washington Gallery of Modern Art, Washington, D.C.

*Concept Tableaux*, Dwan Gallery, New York.

1966    *Anywhere USA*, University of Saskatchewan, Regina, Canada.

*Los Angeles County Museum of Art.

1965    *The Beanery*, Dwan Gallery, New York.

1964    *Three Tableaux* including *Back Seat Dodge '38*, Dwan Gallery, Los Angeles.

1963    Dwan Gallery, Los Angeles.

*Roxys*, Alexander Iolas Gallery, New York.

1962    *A Tableau*, Ferus Gallery, Los Angeles.

1961    Ferus Gallery, Los Angeles.

Pasadena Art Museum.

1960    Ferus Gallery, Los Angeles.

1959    *Collage Constructions (Bengston/Kienholz)*, Ferus Gallery, Los Angeles.

1958    *B.S.*, Exodus Gallery, San Pedro, California.

1956    Syndell Studios, Los Angeles.

1955    Von's Cafe Galeria, Los Angeles.

Coronet Louvre, Los Angeles.

## SELECTED GROUP EXHIBITIONS

2000    *Les Années Pop 1956-1968*, Museé Nationale d'Art Moderne, Centre Georges Pompidou, Paris.

*Ed and Nancy Kienholz & Juhani Harri*, Galerie Forsblom, Helsinki.

*Made in California 1900-2000*, Los Angeles County Museum of Art.

*Berlin segle XX. La coleccio de la Berlinische Galerie*, Ivam Centre Julio Gonzalez, Valencia.

*The New Frontier: Art and Television, 1960-65*, Austin Museum of Art.

*Art in Germany During the XX Century*, Nationalgalerie im Hamburger Bahnhof Museum fur Gegenwart-Berlin.

1999    *Southern California Car Culture*, Irvine Fine Arts Center, California.

1998    *One Hundred Years of Art in Upheaval, The Berlinische Galerie visits Bonn*, Kunst und Ausstellungshalle der Bundesrepublik Deutschland, Bonn.

*From Head to Toe: Concepts of the Body in Twentieth Century Art*, Los Angeles County Museum of Art.

1997    *Magie der Zahl In Der Kunst Des 20. Jahrhunderts*, Staatsgalerie, Stuttgart.

*Shoes or No Shoses? De Voet Van De Verbeelding: Schoenen Als Kunst*, Vishal, Haarlem, Netherlands.

*Tableaux*, Museum of Contemporary Art, Miami; Museum of Contemporary Art, Houston.

*20 Ans, 1977-1997*, Centre Georges Pompidou, Paris.

*Die Epoche der Moderne Kunst im 20. Jahrhundert*, Zeitgeist-Gesellschaft, Berlin.

*Kienholz and Friends*, Redmann Galerie & Verlag, Berlin.

*Finders/Keepers*, Contemporary Arts Museum, Houston.

*Sunshine & Noir, L.A. Art 1960-1997*, The Louisiana Museum of Art, Humlebaek, Denmark; Kunstmuseum Wolfburg, Germany; Castella di Rivoli, Torino, Italy; UCLA at the Armand Hammer Museum of Art, Los Angeles.

1995    *Confronting Nature: Silenced Voices*, Art Gallery, California State University, Fullerton.

**The First Kwangju Biennale*, South Korea.

*Beat Culture and the New America, 1950-1965*, Whitney Museum of American Art, New York; Walker Art Center, Minneapolis; M.H. de Young Memorial Museum, The Fine Arts Museums of San Francisco.

1994    *A Sculpture Show*, Nishimura Gallery, Tokyo.

*Old Glory: The American Flag in Contemporary Art*, Cleveland Center for Contemporary Art.

*Love in the Ruins: Art and the Inspiration of L.A.*, Long Beach Museum of Art, California.

**Of The Human Condition: Hope and Despair at the End of the Century*, Spiral/Wacoal Art Center, Tokyo; Ashiya City Museum of Art and History, Japan.

**Neo-Dada: Redefining Art, 1958-62*, Scottsdale Center for the Arts, Arizona; The Equitable Gallery, New York; Contemporary Arts Museum, Houston; Tuffs University Art Gallery, Medford, Massachusetts; Florida International University Art Museum, Miami.

1993    **Proof: Los Angeles Art and the Photograph 1960-1980*, Laguna Art Museum, California.

*A Salute to the Ferus Gallery*, Norton Simon Museum, Pasadena.

**A Sister City Presentation, Hope in Houston, Houston in Hope*, Moody Gallery, Houston; The Faith and Charity in Hope Gallery, Hope, Idaho.

1992    *Images: Selections from the Lannan Foundation Collection*, Lannan Foundation, Los Angeles.

*Both Art and Life; Gemini at 25*, Newport Harbor Art Museum, Newport Beach, California.

**Territorium Artis*, Kunst und Ausstellungshalle der Bundesrepublik Deutschland, Bonn.

1991    *Cruciformed: Images of the Cross Since 1980*, Cleveland Center for Contemporary Art.

**Pop Art*, The Royal Academy, London, England; Museum Ludwig, Cologne.

1990    *Volksempfängers*, XLIV Venice Biennale.

**Crossing the Line: Word and Image in Art, 1960-1990*, Montgomery Gallery, Pomona College, Claremont, California.

*Berliner Kunst Stücke*, Berlinische Galerie, Berlin.

1989    *Selected Works From The Frederick R. Weisman Art Foundation*, Wight Art Gallery, University of California, Los Angeles.

*The Junk Aesthetic*, Whitney Museum of American Art, New York.

**Masters of The Inland Northwest*, Cheney Cowles Museum, Eastern Washington State Historical Society, Spokane.

*First Impressions*, Walker Art Center, Minneapolis.

*Art in Berlin 1815-1989*, High Museum of Art, Atlanta.

*Art in Berlin 1900*, Centro De Arte Moderna, Lisbon.

**Forty Years of California Assemblage*, The Wight Art Gallery, University of California, Los Angeles; San Jose Museum of Art; Fresno Art Museum; Joslyn Art Museum, Omaha.

1988    **Lost and Found: Four Decades of California Assemblage*, James Corcoran Gallery, Shoshana Wayne Gallery and Pence Gallery, Santa Monica.

*Biennial of Sydney*, Sydney and Melbourne, Australia.

*Committed to Print*, The Museum of Modern Art, New York.

*Sculpture Since the Sixties*, Whitney Museum of American Art, New York.

1987    **Berlinart: 1961-87*, Museum of Modern Art, New York.

*L.A. Hot and Cool: Pioneers*, MIT-List Visual Arts Center, Cambrigde.

*Skulpturenboulevard: Kunst im öffentlichen Raum*, Kurfürstendamm Tauentzen, Berlin.

*Der Unverbrauchte Blick*, Martin Gropius Bau, Berlin.

*Made in U.S.A.: An Americanization in Modern Art: the 50s and 60s*, University Art Museum, University of California, Berkeley.

*10 Jahre Kunst*, Galerie Am Moritzplatz, Berlin.

1986     *Beuys zu Ehren*, Städtische Galerie im Lenbachhaus, Munich.

*T.V. Generations*, Los Angeles Contemporary Exhibitions.

*The Window in Twentieth Century Art*, Neuberger Museum of Art, State University of New York at Purchase; Museum of Contemporary Art, Houston.

*Individuals: A Selected History of Contemporary Art 1945-86*, Inaugural Exhibition, Museum of Contemporary Art, Los Angeles.

1985     *No! Contemporary American DADA*, The Henry Art Gallery, University of Washington, Seattle.

*Transformations in Sculpture: Four Decades of American and European Art*, The Solomon R. Guggenheim Museum, New York.

*Couples: Party of Two*, University Art Gallery, California State University, Chico.

*American Sculpture: Three Decades*, Seattle Art Museum.

*American/European: Painting and Sculpture*, L.A. Louver Gallery, Venice, California.

*Gemini G.E.L.: Art and Collaboration*, Nelson-Atkins Museum of Art, Kansas City.

*Tiden-den 4 Dimension*, The Louisiana Museum, Humlcback, Dcnmark.

1984     *Anxious Interiors: An Exhibition of Tableau Photography and Sculpture*, Laguna Art Museum, California.

*Content: A Contemporary Focus 1974-84*, Hirshhorn Museum and Sculpture Garden, Smithosonian Institution, Washington, D.C.

*Apocalyptic Visions: The Impact of the Bomb in Recent American Art*, Mount Holyoke College, South Hadley, Massachusetts.

*The Human Condition: San Francisco Museum of Modern Art, Biennial III*.

*Narrative Sculpture*, Palm Springs Desert Museum, California.

1983     17th Middelheim Biennial, Antwerp, Belgium.

*American/European: Painting and Sculpture*, L.A. Louver Gallery, Venice, California.

*1933: Wege zur Diktatur*, Staatlische Kunsthalle, Berlin.

*Public Comments*, Center on Contemporary Art, Seattle.

1982     *Art in Los Angeles*: Seventeen Artists in the Sixties, Los Angeles County Museum of Art.

*The Michael and Dorothy Blankfort Collection*, Los Angeles County Museum of Art.

*'60-'80 Attitudes/Concepts/Images*, Stedelijk Museum, Amsterdam.

*Twenty American Artists, Sculpture 1982*, San Francisco Museum of Modern Art.

*One Hundred Years of California Sculpture*, The Oakland Museum.

*Bilder Sind Nich Verboten*, Städtische Kunsthalle, Düsseldorf.

*Tableaux: Nine Contemporary Sculptures*, The Contemporary Arts Center, Cincinnati.

1981     *Visiting Artists Revisited*, University Gallery, University of Idaho, Moscow, Idaho.

*Biennial Exhibition*, Whitney Museum of American Art, New York.

1980     *Ecouter par les yeux: objects et environnements*,

Musée d'Art Moderne de la Ville de Paris.

International Sculpture Conference, Washington, D.C.

*Tableau: An American Selection*, Middendorf/Lane Gallery, Washington, D.C.

1978    *Aspekte der 60er Jahre: Aus der Sammlung Reinhard Onnasch*, Nationalgalerie, Berlin.

1977    Venice Biennale.

1976    *The Last Time I Saw Ferus*, 1957-1966, Newport Harbor Museum, Newport Beach, California.

*Painting and Sculpture in California: The Modern Era*, San Francisco Museum of Modern Art (travelled).

*Two Decades 1957-1977: American Sculpture from Northwest Collections*, Museum of Art, Washington State University, Pullman.

1975    *Eight from Berlin*, Fruit Market Gallery, Scottish Arts Council, Edinburgh.

*Menace*, Museum of Contemporary Art, Chicago.

*Sculpture: American Directions, 1945-1975*, National Collection of Fine Arts, Smithsonian Institution, Washington, D.C.

Galleria Giancarlo Bocchi, Milan.

1974    *Agora 2*, Musée d'Art Moderne, Strasbourg, France.

*Ars '74*, Ateneumin, Taidemuseo, Helsinki.

*Opere principali dal 1961 ad oggi*, Galleria Giancarlo Bocchi, Milan.

1973    *Looking West 1970*, Jocelyn Art Museum, Omaha.

*Record as Artwork*, Françoise Lambert, Milan.

1972    *Documenta V*, Kassel (travelled).

*Surrealism Is Alive and Well in the West*, Baxter Art Gallery, California Institute of Technology, Pasadena.

*West Coast Art from the Permanent Collection*, Pasadena Art Museum.

1971    *Metamorphose van het object*, Musées Royaux des Beaux Arts, Brussels.

*Continuing Surrealism*, La Jolla Museum of Contemporary Art, La Jolla, California.

*The Artist as Adversary*, The Museum of Modern Art, New York.

1970    *Das Ding als Objekt,* Kunsthalle Nürnberg, Nuremberg.

1969    *Kompas 4: West Coast USA*, Stedelijk van Abbe Museum, Eindhoven, The Netherlands.

*Pop Art Redefined*, Hayward Gallery, London.

*Human Concern/Personal Torment: The Grotesque in American Art*, Whitney Museum of American Art, New York.

*Kunst der Sechziger Jahre,* Sammlung Ludwig, Wallraf-Richartz Museum, Cologne.

*When Attitude Becomes Form*, Kunsthalle, Bern, West Germany.

*Ars '69*, Ateneumin Taidemuseum, Helsinki.

1968    *Los Angeles Six*, Vancouver Art Gallery, Canada.

*Late Fifties at the Ferus*, Los Angeles County Museum of Art.

*Documenta 4*, Kassel, West Germany.

*Assemblage in California: Works from the Late 50s and early 60s*, University of California, Irvin.

*The Machine*, The Museum of Modern Art, New York.

*Dada, Surrealism and Their Heritage*, The Museum of Modern Art, New York.

1967    *Protest and Hope*, New School Art Center, New York.

*American Sculpture of the Sixties*, Los Angeles County Museum of Art.

Museum of Modern Art, New York.

1966    *Various Artists*, Dwan Gallery, Los Angeles.

*Sixty-Eighth American Exhibition of Painting and Sculpture*, The Art Institute of Chicago.

*Annual Exhibition of Contemporary Sculpture and*

*Prints*, Whitney Museum of American Art, New York.

1964    *Annual Exhibition of Contemporary American Sculpture*, Whitney Museum of American Art, New York.

**Boxes*, Dwan Gallery, Los Angeles.

1963    *Contemporary California Sculpture*, Oakland Art Museum.

1962    **My Country 'Tis of Thee*, Dwan Gallery, Los Angeles.

*Fifty California Artists*, Whitney Museum of American Art, New York.

1961    *The Art of Assemblage*, The Museum of Modern Art, New York.

1959    *Californians Collect Californians*, Westside Jewish Community Center, Los Angeles.

Ferus Gallery, Los Angeles.

1957    *Ninth San Gabriel Valley Artists Exhibition*, Pasadena Art Museum.

*Objects on the New Landscape Demanding of the Eye*, Ferus Gallery, Los Angeles.

*Pacific Coast Arts Festival*, Reed College, Portland, Oregon.

1956    *Eighth San Gabriel Valley Artist Exhibition*, Pasadena Art Museum.

*Tenth Annual Pacific Northwest Art Exhibition*, Spokane Art Board, Washington.

1955    *Eight Young Artists*, Loyola University, Los Angeles.

## SELECTED PUBLIC COLLECTIONS

Berlinische Galerie das Landesmuseum für Moderne Kunst, Photographie und Architektur, Berlin

Centre national d'art et de culture Georges Pompidou, Paris

Cheney Cowles Museum, Spokane

The Foundation Daniel Templon, Frejus, France

The Frederick R. Weisman Foundation, Los Angeles

The Hirshhorn Museum and Sculpture Garden, Washington, D.C.

J.B. Speed Museum, Louisville

Los Angeles County Museum of Art

The Lousiana Museum, Humlebeak, Denmark

The Ludwig Museum, Cologne, Germany

Menil Collection, Houston

Moderna Museet, Stockholm

Musée d'Epinal, France

Museo de Arte Contemporaneo, Caracas, Venezuela

Museum of Modern Art, New York

Museum of Contemporary Art, Los Angeles

National Museum of American Art, Smithsonian Institution, Washington D.C.

Nationalgalerie, Berlin

Newport Harbor Art Museum, Newport Beach, California

San Francisco Museum of Modern Art, San Francisco

The Sara Hilden Museum, Tampere, Finland

Staatsgalerie Stuttgard, Germany

Stedelijk Museum, Amsterdam

Walker Art Center, Minneapolis

The Whitney Museum of American Art, New York

Photography:
D. James Dee
Philipp Scholz Rittermann
Angelika Weidling

Catalogue Design:
Nae Hayakawa

Production:
Tucker Capparell

Library of Congress Control Number: 2001099046
ISBN: 1-930743-12-2